Quickies
for
Couples

Quickies for Couples

Fast, Fresh Recipes for Two

Katy Scott & Arushi Sinha

CUMBERLAND HOUSE

NASHVILLE, TENNESSEE

QUICKIES FOR COUPLES
PUBLISHED BY CUMBERLAND HOUSE PUBLISHING INC.
431 Harding Industrial Drive
Nashville, Tennessee 37211

Cover design: James Duncan Creative
Text design: Lisa Taylor and Mary Sanford

Library of Congress Cataloging-in-Publication Data
Scott, Katy, 1972–
    Quickies for couples : fast, fresh recipes for two / Katy Scott and Arushi Sinha.
        p. cm.
    Includes index.
    ISBN-13 978-1-58182-347-9 (pbk. : alk. paper)
    ISBN-10 1-58182-347-9 (pbk. : alk. paper)
    1. Cookery for two. 2. Quick and easy cookery. I. Sinha, Arushi, 1972– II. Title.
    TX652.S424 2003
    641.5'61—dc21

                                                                      2003003535

Printed in the United States of America

2 3 4 5 6 7—12 11 10 09 08

This book is dedicated to my husband, Doc, whose lifelong commitment to his music inspired me to work half as hard on something I love; and to Mom, a great teacher who cooks the best food on the planet.

KATY SCOTT

This book is for Mom, who was able to make a full meal at the family's dinner table every evening even though she worked full time. She was always looking for faster ways to do things. And, to my husband, Shyamal, who is always kind, patient, and cheerful, and very adventurous about food, having yet to turn down any of my culinary experiments.

ARUSHI SINHA

Contents

Acknowledgments

We would like to thank the following people for their love, support, recipes, and helpful hints: Murdock Scott, Shyamal Prasad, Jane McCormack, Kathryn Hackett, Shelly Brimer, Susan Hunter, Leslie Lee, Peter Lucchesi, Mike McCormack, Robin Colleen Moore, Colm O'Reagan, Bruce "Trey" Patterson, Kumi & Shashi Prasad, the late Ruby Richardson, Joel Thomas, Bonnie Valant-Spaight, Bob Wright, and Rachel Ziolkowski. Hearty thanks also go to our publisher, Ron Pitkin and the staff at Cumberland House; and last but not least, to Ben & Jerry.

Introduction

Welcome to *Quickies for Couples: Fast, Fresh Recipes for Two*! This is a book not only for partners or couples, but also for roommates, friends, small families, and individuals.

Let's face it: Eating at home can be B - O - R - I - N - G! You should go out to eat from time to time, if only to save yourself the chore of doing dishes for one night, but eating out too often can quickly become cost-prohibitive. What is a time- and money-conscious couple to do?

Quickies for Couples to the rescue! In the pages to come you will find a wide variety of fast and flavorful recipes using only the freshest of readily available ingredients. Most recipes can be prepared in thirty minutes or less, and most are tailored to serve two people. They can easily be doubled if you are really hungry, having company, or just want leftovers. And don't let the romance tips scare you—the resources and recipes in this book will appeal to anyone, whether you're part of a couple, aspiring to be part of one, or happy to be a singleton.

Why "Quickies?"

Well, essentially, because we are tired! We are each half of a busy professional couple, and we have little or no time and energy after work to make the fresh homemade food that we like so much. We're constantly looking for delicious meals that are quick to make and that use fresh, unprocessed ingredients—and that don't leave you eating leftovers for days.

Why "For Couples"?

Katy grew up in a family of five (including two teenage boys who could pack it away like they hadn't eaten for a week) and learned to cook from her mom, who makes the best food on the planet—but in huge quantities. So all the recipes she learned to make would yield enough food for six to eight people.

This obviously does not work very well when you only have two people in your household like we do now (and no huge pans like Mom used). There's only so many days you can eat the leftovers before they lose their appeal, no matter how tasty the dish was to begin with.

We've had to learn how to cook in smaller amounts (and you'd be surprised how difficult an adjustment that is) but we were never able to find much in the way of good cookbooks tailored toward two-person households, not to mention ones that also focused on the "quick" aspect.

So we wrote our own.

What's This About Romance?

In this fast-paced world, it can be hard to get enough quality time alone with our partners, and it's tough to be creative in the romance department when we are so busy. But romance is essential for healthy relationships. "Breaking bread together," sharing meals with our loved ones, is an important tradition that has brought people together since the beginning of time. So we've included in this book some fun romantic menus and tips to help you spark some creative passion of your own!

There is an old saying that we've all heard: "The way to a man's heart is through his stomach." Think about it and you will realize how true it really is, and not just for men either! Eating together is a form of relationship building. Breaking bread is as much a symbolic act as it is a means of filling one's tummy. So it stands to reason that romance and food naturally go together.

Dates occur at restaurants because it gives a couple the chance to share the basic human need for food. It also gives them a space to interact, to exchange stories, and to get to know each other. This is something that is recreated daily, whether on the first date or in the umpteenth year of marriage. Sharing a meal provides both nourishment and an environment for togetherness.

Romance does not have to be a huge-box-of-chocolates, singing-telegram sort of production. Arushi remembers a friend telling her that every Friday afternoon her husband would bring home a pint of her favorite ice cream and a rose.

And while no amount of romance can replace basic politeness (like saying please and thank you), small and meaningful efforts can help make every meal memorable.

What makes a meal romantic? First, it must be eaten together. Take the time to sit down, turn off the TV and the phones and any other beeping elec-

tronic gadgets, and look at each other. Take at least half an hour to actually eat the meal.

Presentation of the food is one part of it. Meals in restaurants are served either in large serving bowls ("family style") or attractively arranged on a plate. You can do the same thing. Something as simple as sprinkling chives or parsley on the rim of the plates can help achieve that professional presentation.

Also, meals can be served in courses. A three-course meal doesn't have to be super-fancy, but it does require that you have the time to eat it. A glass of wine or sparkling water and a simple salad, a pasta entrée, and then fruit for dessert is not necessarily an enormous meal, but it does take time to eat. This is good. This means that you will have to face your partner and think about what to say next, or at least be comfortable with the silences.

Laughing and sharing experiences with your partner is not only fun, it is good for your health. You burned the chicken? So what! Oops, did that batch of pasta accidentally slide down the disposal as you were trying to drain it? That's pretty funny! Cook together, laugh together, and eat together.

And this brings us to the last part of what makes a meal romantic: you have to like to be with your partner. This part you can't fake. This part requires love, dedication, and work both inside and outside of the kitchen.

While we certainly don't expect you to go all-out on a daily basis, try once or twice a week to make your mealtime special. You may be pleasantly surprised at the positive changes this can bring to your relationship.

We hope that the recipes we have provided here will bring you pleasure in the preparation and leave you enough time to enjoy each other's company at the table. These are recipes that come directly from our kitchens to yours, and we delight in the knowledge that they may bring you as much enjoyment and sustenance as they have brought to our families and friends.

And don't forget to say those three little words to your partner every day: "Pass the potatoes!"

Quickies
for
Couples

About the Recipes

What Types of Recipes Will You Find in This Book?

- Flavorful: We have included lots of delicious family recipes (thanks, Mom!) as well as our own favorites that we've gathered and adapted over the years. Don't be afraid of the phrase "family recipe," though, because ours don't include your typical American potluck dishes like ambrosia salad or tuna loaf. These things are "comfort food" to a lot of people, but neither of us grew up with that.
- Fast: Most of the recipes can be prepared in thirty minutes or less. Some do take a little more time, but we think the results are well worth it. And most are tailored to serve two people but can be easily doubled, tripled, or halved.
- Friendly: We present the recipes in plain English, with easy-to-follow bulleted instructions. You'll also find a list of the necessary kitchen equipment with each recipe. And check out the Resources section for quick mix-and-match charts!
- Fresh: We avoid processed food as much as possible, so our recipes use simple fresh ingredients and spices. The fewer preservatives you put into your body, the better. In fact, the only canned or processed things that we generally keep as staples in our own pantries are canned tomatoes and beans, dried pasta, and chicken broth. Everything else comes fresh. It's easier than you think!

With each recipe we have listed the kitchen equipment that you will need to complete that dish. However, to avoid unnecessarily long lists, we do not include basics such as wooden spoons, sharp knives, cutting boards, measuring utensils, plastic zipper bags and tinfoil, serving dishes, microwave, stove, oven, and refrigerator.

We do tell you when you need bowls, pans, baking sheets, non-basic utensils such as rolling pins or pastry brushes, and equipment like blenders and electric mixers.

Ingredients are listed in the order in which you use them the each recipe. Almost all ingredients we use are easily found in most major supermarkets. If something is a little unusual, we tell you where to look for it.

While most of these recipes are tailored for two people, a number of them do yield more servings. These are typically things like appetizers, salad dressings, and desserts: things that you would be most likely to make when you have company (and thus need to feed more people) or recipes whose leftovers keep or freeze well (such as chili, pasta sauce, or salad dressing). You can always cut the ingredients in any recipe in half or thirds, but keep in mind that a partial recipe may need less cooking or baking time than called for.

We hope you enjoy these dishes as much as we do. And we hope that you find the Resources section especially helpful.

Why Did We Write This Cookbook?

The idea to write this book sparked in Katy's brain during a career identity crisis, one of those "I'm almost thirty and I still don't know what I want to be when I grow up" moments.

While idly leafing through one of her *Southern Living* annuals to find something to make for dinner one night, it occurred to her that it might be a really fun job to work for a company that put together these books. You know—gathering recipes, testing them, and writing and designing a book around them.

That job, if it existed, would make use of her passions for cooking (and eating!), writing, computers, and art all at once.

The more practical side of her, though, said that no one person working for a cookbook publishing company got to do all of those things. When Arushi heard about her musings, she agreed and said, "We have lots of recipes. Why don't we try to write a cookbook of our own?"

Well, it seemed like a great way to get experience in every aspect of cookbook writing from start to finish, so we started putting together ideas, testing recipes on our friends and family, and writing down what our extensive practical kitchen experience had taught us. A handy hint: if you are in the market for a lot of free meals, just get someone you know to write a cookbook!

A Note About Cookbooks

Cookbooks are always a work in progress, and no ingredient list is ever set in stone. Recipes can be changed to suit your tastes, your needs, and your budget. Although we both own lots of cookbooks, there are hardly any recipes that we follow "by the book." Invariably we'll modify a recipe to make it our own, writing notes in the margins. Our favorite recipes are those that we have personalized.

We hope that you will think about our recipes in this way. Feel free to adapt them to your requirements, and please let us know when you do. We 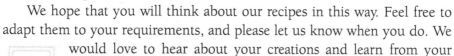 would love to hear about your creations and learn from your efforts. You can find us on the Web at *www.quickiesforcouples.com*.

Resources

Basic Kitchen Equipment

To prepare most of the dishes in this book (and pretty much anything else that isn't too fancy), you need some very basic items in your kitchen. Most of these things can be purchased in varying degrees of quality from a kitchen specialty store, a large bed/bath/kitchen supply store, or even all-purpose discount stores such as Target. You can get anything from the 99-cent plastic version of an item to somewhat more expensive but sturdier versions made of steel, glass, marble, teflon, pyrex, etc. Remember that higher-quality items look and feel better, and are built to last. If you are just starting out, you can get the cheap versions of these items and replace them with better quality ones as you develop a feel for what you like. If you have everything on the list below, you are prepared to make almost any recipe!

Quality kitchen gadgets also make great gift ideas. (Romance tip: but maybe not for anniversary presents!) For a festive presentation, try wrapping nice utensils such as olivewood spoons and silicone spatulas in red and green tissue paper like long-stemmed roses, and place them in a nice heavy ceramic or stainless steel container.

THE MOST BASIC EQUIPMENT: BUY THE BEST YOU CAN AFFORD

These are the only two things Arushi started out with. If you have nothing else, spend your precious money on these two basic things:

- A good quality chef's knife. I use a Henckels knife and paid about sixty dollars for it (ouch!), but it has been worth every penny and is easily resharpened. A knife sharpening steel costs about forty dollars.
- A good quality 2-quart saucepan with a lid (one that is made of several layers, usually an aluminum core in a stainless steel sandwich). You will rarely

burn food, and it cleans up easily. I use All-Clad pans, but any similarly constructed pan will work.

OTHER BASIC EQUIPMENT: THESE ITEMS WILL COMPLETE ANY KITCHEN

- Two more saucepans (1- and 4-quart) with lids
- Paring knife
- Mixing bowls in varying sizes (6-inch, 8-inch, 10-inch)
- Two wooden spoons (rounded end and flat end)
- Rubber or silicone spatula
- Whisk
- Large slotted spoon
- Pancake turner, or other wide and flat utensil
- Set of measuring cups
- Set of measuring spoons
- Two cutting boards (one for meat, one for everything else)
- Two non-stick skillets (small and large) with lids if possible
- Two baking sheets—nonstick are the best
- Metal tongs
- Two wire cooling racks
- 8-inch square glass baking dish
- Cheese grater
- Vegetable peeler
- Colander or strainer
- Juicer (the little pointed dome that you squeeze citrus fruit against)
- Can opener
- Corkscrew
- Pot holders
- Aluminum foil (roll or sheets)
- Plastic wrap
- Various food storage equipment (plastic zipper bags, plastic refrigerator containers)
- Clips or clothespins for keeping bags closed

NICE EXTRAS

- Meat mallet
- Ladle
- Rolling pin
- Bread loaf pans
- 9 x 13-inch glass baking dish
- Two 8-inch or 9-inch round metal cake pans
- Blender and/or food processor
- Electric hand mixer or stand mixer (the kind with the bowl attached)
- Small chopper (great for fast cooking and for Speedy Guacamole, p. 59)
- Microwave oven
- Electric wok

We assume that you already have plates and bowls, glasses, flatware, an oven, a gas or electric stove, a refrigerator, and a freezer.

Basic Pantry Staples

Don't be overwhelmed by these lists of supplies! A well-stocked kitchen is a work in progress, and you may only buy one or two things on the list each time you head out to the grocery store. Depending upon your tastes, you might end up needing only a few items from each category. More likely, though, you'll find that you will want to stock most, if not all, of the basic things listed below.

BAKING

- white flour (unbleached)
- white sugar
- brown sugar (light)
- powdered or confectioner's sugar
- baking soda
- cocoa powder
- semisweet chocolate chips
- shortening (regular or butter-flavored)
- yeast (active dry—watch the expiration date)
- cornstarch

OILS/SAUCES

- balsamic vinegar
- white vinegar
- soy sauce
- Sherry cooking wine
- Worcestershire sauce
- olive oil
- canola or blended vegetable oil

CANNED GOODS

- canned pinto or white beans
- canned black beans
- canned diced tomatoes
- tomato paste
- canned chicken broth (or vegetable broth)

RICE/PASTA

- angel hair pasta (or your favorite kind of string pasta)
- shell or rotini pasta (or your favorite kind of shaped pasta)
- rice (have on hand both plain white and a more flavorful kind, such as Basmati or brown)

SPICES

- salt
- ground black pepper (or pep-percorns if you have a mill)
- garlic salt or garlic powder
- fresh garlic cloves
- oregano
- basil
- rosemary
- ground ginger
- cinnamon
- ground cumin
- chili powder
- bouillon (chicken or vegetable)
- vanilla extract
- Tabasco sauce (or your favorite hot pepper sauce)

OTHER SPICES (NICE TO HAVE, BUT NOT ESSENTIAL FOR MOST RECIPES)

- thyme
- paprika
- turmeric
- allspice
- nutmeg
- MSG (sold under the brand name Accént)
- dry mustard
- seeds (sesame, poppy, fennel, caraway)
- cayenne pepper

BEVERAGES

- bottled or filtered water
- sparkling water or soft drinks
- your favorite beer
- your favorite wine, both red and white
- teabags
- ground coffee

Basic Refrigerator/Freezer Staples

DAIRY/EGGS

- milk (skim, 2 percent, or whichever kind you prefer)
- plain yogurt (nonfat or lowfat)
- butter or margarine (butter is best)
- sour cream
- your favorite kind of cheeses (remember: harder cheeses keep longer than softer cheeses)
- eggs

FRESH SPICES

- ginger
- cilantro
- hot green chilies (such as jalapeño or serrano)

FRUITS

- berries in season (such as strawberries or raspberries)
- apples
- oranges
- lemons and/or limes

VEGETABLES

- tomatoes
- leafy greens (spinach, bok choy, mixed salad greens, etc)
- zucchini and/or yellow squash
- bell pepper (red, yellow, green)
- yellow onions
- button mushrooms
- carrots (regular or baby)
- potatoes

BREAD

- a hearty loaf such as a French baguette or other "specialty" bakery bread
- sliced whole wheat or white
- tortillas (flour or corn)

FREEZER

- frozen peas
- frozen corn
- frozen orange juice concentrate
- your favorite kind of ice cream!

MEAT

- Chicken breasts or tenders, or pork cutlets. Buy in the family-size packages (less expensive per pound), and as fresh as you can get them. Rinse them in cool water and pat dry on paper towels. Place each individual piece of meat (2 or 3 for chicken tenders) in a quart-size plastic freezer bag, flatten with your hand, seal, and stack in the freezer. This is a great storage method for using only one or two pieces at a time instead of thawing the entire package of meat. Be sure to label each bag with the date.
- Ground beef. Use the same method as above, dividing beef into 4-ounce portions and flattening in the bags to ¼-inch thick rounds. You can put the frozen patties directly on the grill to cook as hamburgers, or thaw and use the meat for other recipes.
- Shrimp and fish. Although it is preferable to buy shrimp and fish fresh and use them within two days of purchase, they can be frozen for future use. Be sure they are wrapped securely in plastic, then place into a paper sack or wrap in waxed paper and label with the date.

Common Sense Cooking Tips

FIRE SAFETY

- Never leave the house while the stove, oven, or microwave are on.
- Turn dish handles and spoons away from the edge of the stove.
- Don't overheat oil. It will catch fire (Katy knows this from a tragic family experience). Do not throw water on an oil fire! Use baking soda or a fire extinguisher—and call the fire department immediately if it doesn't go completely out within a few seconds.
- Keep a fire extinguisher in your kitchen, but away from the stove. Know how to use it, and test/recharge it regularly.
- Do not store flammable objects (such as oil or matches) above or near the stove or oven.

FOOD SAFETY

- "Washing" food like fruits or vegetables means rinse only! Do not use soap.

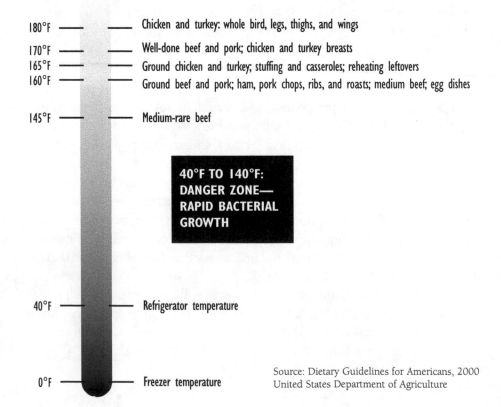

180°F — Chicken and turkey: whole bird, legs, thighs, and wings

170°F — Well-done beef and pork; chicken and turkey breasts
165°F — Ground chicken and turkey; stuffing and casseroles; reheating leftovers
160°F — Ground beef and pork; ham, pork chops, ribs, and roasts; medium beef; egg dishes

145°F — Medium-rare beef

40°F TO 140°F: DANGER ZONE— RAPID BACTERIAL GROWTH

40°F — Refrigerator temperature

0°F — Freezer temperature

Source: Dietary Guidelines for Americans, 2000
United States Department of Agriculture

- The safest way to defrost or marinate meat is in the refrigerator, not on the countertop.
- Cook food to a safe temperature. (See the chart on the previous page.)
- Store foods at the proper recommended temperature. Make sure that your refrigerator is at or below 40°F, and that the freezer is at or below 0°F.
- Not sure if it's still good? When in doubt, throw it out!
- Devein shrimp (see technique, p. 40).
- Rinse chicken pieces under cool water before using.
- Wash your hands before you start any work in the kitchen.
- Wash your hands and utensils thoroughly after handling meat. Put the utensils into the dishwasher.
- Keep a separate cutting board for meat (including poultry, fish, and eggs). Wash it with a diluted bleach solution after use (2 tablespoons per quart of water—store in a labeled bottle), or put it into the dishwasher.
- Wipe down counters with the diluted bleach solution. This will kill most bacteria.
- Put the dishwashing sponge and sponge holder into the dishwasher once a week, and soak regularly in the diluted bleach solution.
- Wash kitchen towels regularly.

A NOTE ABOUT ALLERGIES

- Monosodium glutamate (MSG) causes an intolerance reaction in some people. Symptoms include burning sensations, chest and facial flushing and pain, and throbbing headaches. See your doctor if you experience these symptoms.
- Some ingredients listed in our recipes are among the more common allergy-causing foods, such as shellfish, peanuts, and dairy products. However, people can be allergic to just about anything. For instance, we have a friend who can't eat citrus fruits, garlic, tomatoes, or chocolate. (And we all sympathize with his plight as we scarf down Italian meals and chocolate cake.) If you are allergic to ingredients in particular recipes, please make your own substitutions or avoid the recipes altogether. Hives and other allergic reactions are not conducive to romance.

OTHER SAFETY

- Keep knife handles and blades away from the edge of countertops.
- Keep knives sharp. Dull knives can slip and cause you to cut yourself.

SMART SHOPPING

- Do not shop for groceries on an empty stomach! When you're hungry, everything looks good and you tend to buy more (and if you're like us, more junk food) than you would if you'd eaten before you shopped.
- Stick to the outside perimeter and aisles of the store. Processed foods tend to be located nearer the center of the store.
- Read labels on everything and check expiration dates.
- Bag your meat, poultry, and fish in plastic.
- Check cans for dents and bulges.
- Check packaging for tears or openings.
- Keep a small styrofoam chest in the car, especially during the summer. This will help keep your frozen foods frozen on the way home.
- Generic-brand goods are often identical to their brand-name counterparts and have a lower price. This is not true of all products, so test them and see what you like.
- Buy food as fresh as possible, especially meats and spices.
- Buy spices in smaller amounts to keep them potent. Buy them whole and grind them at home, or get in bulk as needed.
- Buying spices in bulk (for instance, spooning the desired amount out of a jar at the organic food market) is usually shockingly less expensive than getting the standard-size jars at the supermarket.
- Ethnic food markets are great places to get items such as rice, meat, and spices, and they are usually a great deal less expensive than the supermarket, too.

COOKING TIPS

- Keep a small, easily washable (glass or steel) bowl for cuttings and peelings. This will save those thousands of trips to the wastebasket or the compost pile.
- If you have a yard, starting a compost pile can be as simple as reserving a corner of your garden for scraps. Check with your city's sanitation department for tips and regulations.
- When frying foods in oil, keep a small bowl of white vinegar sitting nearby to cut down on the smell.
- Wash dishes as you go while preparing a meal. This keeps cleanup from being overwhelming when you are done and provides you more space to work.
- Store garlic on the pantry shelf or in a small clay pot made expressly for this purpose. Don't keep it in the refrigerator.

- Line the bottom of fruit and vegetable bins in your refrigerator with paper towels. This will cut down on excess moisture.
- For more flavor, crush dried herbs between your fingers before adding them to a dish.
- Never soak wooden-handled knives (or other wooden-handled utensils). Wash and dry them quickly. Soaking swells the handle and can warp and separate it from the metal. Scrub wooden cutting boards well after each use, and then wipe dry. Leaving water on them can lead to cracking. Also, every few months, rub them with vegetable oil and leave overnight.
- Set your oven rack in the lower half of the oven, unless you are broiling or have a convection oven.
- When steaming vegetables, steam only until crisp-tender, and when finished, plunge immediately into a bowl of ice water to stop the cooking process. This locks in the bright color and fresh flavor.

HOW TO KNEAD DOUGH

- This is a general guide; your recipe's instructions may differ.
  1. Thoroughly wash and dry your hands.
  2. Prepare a clean and dry countertop or wooden cutting board by sprinkling flour over the surface (lightly or liberally, depending on the recipe). Lightly flour your hands, as well.
  3. Scoop the ball of dough out of the mixing bowl, and plop it on the floured surface.
  4. Press the heels of your hands into the dough at an angle away from you. Move the sides of your hands to the top corners of the dough and scoop it over the top toward you, folding it over on itself. Again press the heels of your hands into the dough, and repeat the cycle in a nice steady rhythm. After eight or ten pushes, pick up the dough and plop it onto the counter at a different angle. Start the kneading process again.
  5. Continue kneading and scooping and changing the orientation of the dough until it is nicely smooth and elastic, or whatever your recipe instructs.
  6. You may occasionally need to sprinkle additional flour on the surface, depending on the consistency of your dough.
- After yeast dough has been kneaded, it usually needs to be left alone to rise at least once. Some recipes call for letting the dough rise twice.
  1. Oil or grease the bottom and sides of a clean large bowl.

2. Place the dough in the bowl, and cover it with a kitchen towel. Place the bowl in a warm, non-drafty place for about an hour to an hour and a half, or whatever your recipe calls for. It will double in size during this time. Good places to let dough rise (especially during colder months) are inside a gas oven with the pilot light only or an electric oven with just the light bulb on.

3. When it is time to continue, remove the dough from the bowl onto a clean counter and "punch down"—literally give it a few soft punches with your fists to deflate it. During the rising process, the yeast gives off lots of carbon dioxide, and the thousands of tiny bubbles are what make the dough inflate.

GREASING AND FLOURING PANS

1. Slip your hand inside a plastic sandwich bag, and scoop out a small amount of shortening or butter. Rub the shortening all around the pan, being sure to work it into all corners and edges. You can keep the plastic bag in the shortening container for future use.

2. If you also need to flour the pan, place 1 to 2 tablespoons of flour in the bottom of the pan. Pick up the pan and shake the flour all around until it coats the bottom. Hold the pan at an angle so the flour falls onto one of the sides of the pan. Tap the bottom to get the excess to fall. By turning and tapping the pan in the palm of your other hand or on the counter, move the flour along all sides of the pan until it is completely coated in flour. Dump the excess into the next pan to be floured, or into the trash.

• The easiest way to remove baked goods (such as cakes) from baking pans is to place a wire cooling rack (or even a dinner plate) upside down on the pan, then flip the whole thing over. Tap the bottom of the pan to get the cake to fall out onto the rack.

OTHER KITCHEN TIPS

• Don't let bread, milk, and other perishables touch refrigerator walls— they may freeze.

• Always add croutons to a salad at the last possible moment to prevent sogginess.

• Spices and herbs keep best in a cool dark place. Exposure to excessive light or moisture can ruin the flavor.

• Rinse berries and mushrooms just before using. Rinsing too far ahead of time will make them mushy.

- You don't need as much salt or seasoning in hot food as you do in cold food.
- Grill or bake chicken with the skin on, then remove the skin when you are eating it. The chicken will be juicier and more flavorful, with little added fat.
- Warm all dishes and platters that will be used for hot food by putting them in the oven on the lowest setting. This helps keep the food warm as it is served.
- Do not store milk in the refrigerator door. It stays colder if kept on a shelf.
- Discard soft cheeses when moldy because the mold can penetrate through them.
- Cover your butter with a sheet of plastic wrap or keep in an enclosed butter keeper.
- Don't store chopped onions in the refrigerator—always chop just before using. Even in a tightly sealed container, the smell will quickly permeate your entire refrigerator.
- If your soup, stew, or sauce is overly salty, add a raw potato half and continue cooking to absorb the salt.
- Be sure to thoroughly rinse all leafy greens, such as spinach or cilantro—they can trap dirt and grit. A salad spinner is a great device for this purpose (OXO makes a great one).

Mix and Match Charts

Salads

Greens need to be rinsed and patted dry—a salad spinner is real time-saver. They may then be torn by hand into bite-sized pieces or sliced into shreds with a knife. Unless you plan to serve the salad immediately, don't use a metal knife because it will cause the edges of the greens to quickly turn brown. Sharp plastic knives specifically for cutting lettuce are available at kitchen supply stores.

Start with a salad bowl sized to serve the number of people who will be eating the salad. Choose one or more items from the greens column and toss in the bowl. Then pile on any number of items from the veggies and extras column, and toss the salad if you wish. The quantity of each item depends entirely on your taste.

Salads and their ingredients are most flavorful when served cool but near room temperature.

Dressing can be added and tossed in with the salad if you plan to serve it immediately, or passed separately at the table. If you are calorie-conscious, keep a ramekin of dressing next to your salad plate and dip your empty fork into the dressing before spearing each bite of salad. This cuts down tremendously on the amount of dressing you will consume.

Salads are always delicious served with a slice of crusty bread to sop up extra dressing.

MIX-AND-MATCH SALADS		
Greens: Choose one or more	**Veggies: choose as many as you like**	**Extras: choose as many as you like**
Spinach (curly leaf, flat leaf, or baby)	Sliced mushrooms	Freshly cooked spiral or shell pasta
Iceberg lettuce	Thinly sliced or shredded carrots	Diced cooked potatoes
Mixed field greens (often called "mesclun mix")	Sliced radishes	Chopped hard-boiled eggs
Romaine lettuce	Cherry tomatoes	Kalamata olives
Red or green leaf lettuce	Diced tomatoes	Drained sun-dried tomatoes
Butter lettuce	Sliced onions	Chopped, sliced, or shredded chicken or turkey
Cabbage (green, red, or napa)	Sliced green onions	Crumbled bacon
Arugula	Peas	Honey-roasted peanuts
Kale	Corn	Dry-roasted peanuts
Swiss chard	Sliced cucumbers	Cheese (blue, feta, Cheddar, Monterey Jack, Parmesan, etc.)
	Sliced zucchini	Canned pinto or black beans (drained)
	Broccoli florets	Broken tortilla chips
	Sliced celery	Mandarin orange sections
	Chopped fresh cilantro	Sliced strawberries
	Bell pepper, any color	Croutons
		Edible flowers (found in the produce section of some supermarkets)
		Dressing (see recipes starting on p. 145)

QUICK MIX-AND-MATCH SALAD IDEAS

- *Mom's Classic Salad:* Iceberg lettuce, sliced red cabbage, sliced mushrooms, shredded carrots, sliced radishes, cherry tomatoes, and croutons; served with Thousand Island Dressing (see p. 152) on the side.
- *Spinach Pesto Pasta Salad:* Mixed baby spinach and field greens, cooked shell pasta tossed with pesto, sliced red and yellow bell peppers, diced cooked potatoes, Kalamata olives, grilled chicken or shrimp, crumbled bacon, Parmesan cheese, and croutons; tossed with balsamic vinaigrette dressing.
- *Greek Salad:* Green leaf lettuce, sliced cucumbers, Kalamata olives, sun-dried tomatoes, and feta cheese; tossed with Lighter Lemon Vinaigrette (see p. 149).
- *Summer Salad:* Flat-leaf or baby spinach, sliced green onions, sliced strawberries, mandarin orange sections, shredded cooked chicken breast, and honey-roasted pecans; tossed with Poppy Seed Dressing (see p. 150). Especially beautiful with edible flowers sprinkled on top.
- More salad recipes can be found starting on p. 133.

Pizza

Pizza, in our opinion, is one of life's most perfect delicacies. It can contain all the food groups—breads/grains, vegetables, fruits, meats, and dairy. Generally loaded with cheese and meat, a calorie-rich pizza is not always the best meal to eat on a regular basis (especially delivery pizza). But if you create your pizza wisely, it can be part of a healthy diet.

Cheeseless pizza doesn't sound appealing to a lot of people, but it is becoming widely available in restaurants as a healthy alternative to the traditional. And as cheese is one of the "pitfalls" of pizza—containing huge amounts of calories—a pizza without cheese certainly qualifies as a healthier choice.

But if you are like us, pizza just isn't pizza without cheese. Our solution is to merely cut down on the amount of cheese we use. You still get good flavor without a lot of extra calories. And then when you do occasionally indulge in a slice of Extra Cheese, you don't need to feel guilty about it.

The other calorie trap in pizza is meat. Pepperoni, sausage, and beef are surefire ways to add to your waistline. Try sticking with healthier meats, like Canadian bacon, shrimp, lowfat smoked sausage, or chicken. If you use the higher-fat meats, try using them sparingly as "seasoning" to complement the other toppings.

Almost anything in the world can go on pizza—be creative! Look

MIX-AND-MATCH PIZZA

Crusts	Sauces and Seasonings	Toppings
Traditional white crust (such as Boboli) Katy's Grilled Pizza Crusts (see p. 68) Whole wheat crust Thick pita bread Tortillas Portobello Mushroom Caps (see p. 119) Party-size rye bread Triscuit crackers Hoagie sandwich rolls or horizontally sliced French bread	Alfredo sauce Marinara sauce Tomato paste Katy's Garlic Mushroom Red Sauce (see p. 117) Olive oil and garlic Basil pesto Barbecue sauce Hoisin sauce Oregano (dried or fresh) Basil (dried or fresh) Thyme (dried or fresh) Italian seasoning blend Salt Garlic salt Black pepper Cayenne pepper	All meats should be fully cooked before going on the pizza. Pepperoni Sliced smoked sausage Crumbled Italian sausage Canadian bacon Ground beef Sautéed shrimp Sliced chicken breast Sliced mushrooms Sliced tomatoes Sliced or chopped bell peppers Green or Kalamata olives Pineapple Steamed broccoli Artichoke hearts Sun-dried tomatoes Garlic (roasted or fresh) Sliced onions Cheese (Parmesan, Cheddar, Mozzarella, Monterey or Pepper Jack, smoked Gouda, etc.)

through your refrigerator and pantry and try to spot things that might taste good on a crust. You might be surprised at what you can come up with!

Handy pizza hint: Ever wonder how they make those "gourmet" pizzas? Simple! They heat up all the toppings first and then bake them on the pizza. For instance, briefly sauté your favorite ingredients (veggies, olives, cooked meats) in a bit of olive oil, sprinkle onto your tomato-sauced pizza crust, and bake.

QUICK MIX-AND-MATCH PIZZA IDEAS

- *Traditional Cheese Pizza:* Traditional white crust, tomato paste, oregano, basil, thyme, salt, pepper, Parmesan cheese, Mozzarella cheese.
- *Vegetarian Gourmet:* Whole wheat crust, olive oil, minced garlic, oregano, basil, thyme, salt, cayenne pepper, mushrooms, artichoke hearts, sun-dried tomatoes, sliced red bell peppers, Kalamata olives, smoked Gouda cheese.
- *White Basil Pizza:* Herbed pizza crust, alfredo sauce, salt and pepper, basil pesto or fresh basil leaves, thinly sliced chicken breast, thinly sliced tomatoes, Monterey Jack cheese.
- *Quick Cracker Pizza:* Triscuit crackers, marinara sauce, sliced pepperoni, Mozzarella cheese. These can be easily and successfully microwaved.
- *Asian Shrimp Pizza:* Crust of your choice, hoisin sauce, cooked and shelled shrimp, pineapple, sliced green onions, Monterey Jack cheese (optional). Serve with Teriyaki Sauce (p. 155) or Creamy Teriyaki Sauce (p. 153) for dipping.

Pasta

If we were trapped on a deserted island and could eat only one meal for the rest of our lives (presuming, of course, that the island had a well-stocked kitchen and garden), it would probably be a bowl of hot pasta with fresh tomato sauce and Parmesan cheese, a green salad, a slice of crusty garlic bread, and a glass of wine. This meal is simple, healthy, and fast.

Sauces made with tomatoes are often the quickest and healthiest. This is quite a happy coincidence, because tomatoes are rich in antioxidants and vitamins A and C, and are fabulous for your health. Research shows that eating lots of tomatoes may even lower your risk for certain types of cancer.

Canned tomatoes also have nearly as many nutrients as fresh (and the canning process doesn't destroy the antioxidant properties), so don't feel bad about using them if you don't have immediate access to fresh tomatoes. Keep in mind, though, that canned tomatoes usually have more salt than fresh. Look for a no-salt-added variety.

But tomato sauces are certainly not the only things with which you can adorn pasta. Very popular is the cheese-and-cream concoction known as Alfredo sauce. And something as simple as olive oil and garlic can create a superb dish.

When cooking pasta, make sure that the water is at a nice rolling boil before adding the dried pasta. It's OK, but not necessary, to add salt or oil to the cooking water. Stir while cooking to prevent the pasta from sticking

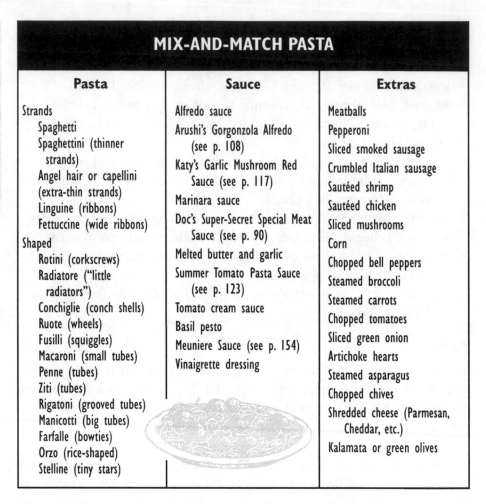

MIX-AND-MATCH PASTA		
Pasta	**Sauce**	**Extras**

Strands
  Spaghetti
  Spaghettini (thinner
    strands)
  Angel hair or capellini
    (extra-thin strands)
  Linguine (ribbons)
  Fettuccine (wide ribbons)
Shaped
  Rotini (corkscrews)
  Radiatore ("little
    radiators")
  Conchiglie (conch shells)
  Ruote (wheels)
  Fusilli (squiggles)
  Macaroni (small tubes)
  Penne (tubes)
  Ziti (tubes)
  Rigatoni (grooved tubes)
  Manicotti (big tubes)
  Farfalle (bowties)
  Orzo (rice-shaped)
  Stelline (tiny stars)
	Alfredo sauce
	Arushi's Gorgonzola Alfredo
	  (see p. 108)
	Katy's Garlic Mushroom Red
	  Sauce (see p. 117)
	Marinara sauce
	Doc's Super-Secret Special Meat
	  Sauce (see p. 90)
	Melted butter and garlic
	Summer Tomato Pasta Sauce
	  (see p. 123)
	Tomato cream sauce
	Basil pesto
	Meuniere Sauce (see p. 154)
	Vinaigrette dressing
		Meatballs
		Pepperoni
		Sliced smoked sausage
		Crumbled Italian sausage
		Sautéed shrimp
		Sautéed chicken
		Sliced mushrooms
		Corn
		Chopped bell peppers
		Steamed broccoli
		Steamed carrots
		Chopped tomatoes
		Sliced green onion
		Artichoke hearts
		Steamed asparagus
		Chopped chives
		Shredded cheese (Parmesan,
		  Cheddar, etc.)
		Kalamata or green olives

together and to prevent the water from boiling over. Cook only until al dente (tender, but still firm to the bite). You determine this by tasting it at various points while it cooks. When it's ready, drain the pasta in a colander (do not rinse), transfer it to a bowl, and add a small amount of butter or olive oil, tossing to coat. Keep the pasta warm in an oven set on low until it's ready to serve, or place in the refrigerator for chilled dishes.

QUICK MIX-AND-MATCH PASTA IDEAS

- *Doc's Chicken Scampi Pasta:* Angel hair pasta, chicken breast strips cooked in butter and garlic, parmesan cheese.
- *Alfredo Primavera:* Fettuccine, Arushi's Gorgonzola Alfredo sauce (p. 108), diced cooked ham, steamed broccoli.

- *Baked Rigatoni:* Rigatoni, Doc's Super-Secret Special Meat Sauce (p. 90), sliced mushrooms, grated Mozzarella cheese. Bake in a casserole dish at 375°F for 30 minutes.
- *Basic Pasta Salad:* Chilled rotini, vinaigrette dressing, artichoke hearts, chopped tomatoes, shrimp.

Sandwiches

It is commonly believed that the word *sandwich* originated with English nobleman John Montague, the fourth Earl of Sandwich, in the 1700s. He was an avid gambler, and often ate meat placed neatly between slices of bread while playing, thus leaving his hands grease-free for handling cards. This apparently caught on and the meal became known, appropriately enough, as a "sandwich." Of course, people were actually eating the equivalent of sandwiches long before the Earl popularized the name. It was common for field workers and travelers to carry meat between slices of bread as a convenience. And other civilizations have always stuffed their tortillas, pitas, and breads with various fillings.

Today, the sandwich remains one of the easiest, tastiest, and most infinitely variable quick meals that exists. It is by far the most popular lunch item in America—look at the enormous variety of sandwich and sub shops. And what kid doesn't scarf down countless peanut butter and jelly sandwiches?

If you are packing a sandwich for lunch, try packing the ingredients separately in plastic zipper bags or containers. You can also use 2-ounce disposable plastic portion cups for condiments. It takes a little more time in preparation, but we have found that it is well worth it for a fresh-tasting sandwich. There's nothing yuckier than a soggy sandwich where the mayonnaise has leaked through the bread or the lettuce has wilted.

If you are eating sandwiches for lunch day after day, they are bound to get boring sooner or later. But there are ways to make them interesting: try heating up a ham and cheese sandwich, for instance. Or add chopped seeded jalapeño peppers for a tangy, spicy shock to the mouth. Sautéed onions are always good for variety, and you can even revive that delicious childhood practice of adding chips directly into the sandwich!

Prepackaged lunchmeat is quite convenient, but not always the most nutritious sandwich topping due to the preservatives used in it. Try getting meats sliced at the deli counter, or ideally use leftovers from another meal.

Remember: you can stuff pretty much anything inside a tortilla or between slices of bread! And, just like "gourmet" pizza ingredients, they can be sautéed to give an entirely different set of flavors.

MIX-AND-MATCH SANDWICHES

Bread	Spreads	Filling
Hearty white bread	Mayonnaise	Lunchmeat slices (ham, turkey, roast beef, bologna, salami, pastrami, corned beef)
Whole wheat bread	Mustard (a few of the popular ones are yellow, brown, spicy, honey mustard, sweet and hot, English, ale mustard, Dijon, and "Dijonnaise")	Meat leftovers (sliced ham, turkey, roast beef, chicken, pork, sausage, meatballs, hamburger, shrimp, fish)
Rye or pumpernickel		
Braided Scarborough Fair Bread (see p. 64)		
Debra's Simple Beer Bread (see p. 66)		
Tortillas (plain or flavored) for rolling up or folding in half	Butter	Tuna, chicken, or egg salad
	Cream cheese	Cheese (Cheddar, Swiss, American, Jack, Muenster, Provolone, pimiento cheese spread, etc.)
	Sour cream	
Pocket bread (pita bread)	Relish (pickle or other)	
Flatbread	Barbecue sauce	Bacon
Hamburger buns	Ketchup	Lettuce, spinach, or any other greens
Hot dog buns	Horseradish or horseradish sauce	
Hoagie or sub rolls		Shredded carrots
Crackers (for tiny, crunchy sandwiches)	Salad dressing (Italian, creamy Italian, Ranch, Thousand Island, Russian, Caesar, blue cheese, vinaigrette, etc.)	Tomato slices
		Onions (raw or sautéed)
Bagels		Cucumber slices
Any sort of roll or bun	Chutney	Bell peppers (fresh or sautéed)
	Salsa	Sprouts
	Hummous	Avocado slices or guacamole
	Any sort of dip or spread	Mushrooms, sliced
	Peanut butter	Jalapeño peppers, sliced
	Jelly	Sun-dried tomatoes
	Honey	Pickles (sweet or dill)
		Potato chips (or your favorite kind of chip)
		Artichoke hearts
		Olives
		Nuts (peanuts, cashews, almonds, sunflower seeds, etc.)
		Dried or fresh fruit slices

QUICK MIX-AND-MATCH SANDWICH IDEAS

- *Katy's Peanut Butter and Pickle* (not everyone's favorite, but I love them): Whole wheat bread, peanut butter, mayonnaise, sliced sweet or dill pickles.
- *Classic Grilled Cheese:* Hearty white bread, butter, Cheddar cheese. Spread both sides of the bread with butter, put the cheese between bread, grill in a skillet on medium heat until nicely browned on both sides and the cheese is melted. (College student version: wrap sandwich securely in foil and press both sides with a hot iron for a few minutes until melted!)
- *Italian Veggie Roll-Up:* Large tortilla (9-inch to 12-inch), spinach, green onions, sun-dried tomatoes, artichoke hearts, red bell pepper, mushrooms, Provolone cheese, creamy Italian dressing.
- *Tiny Tuna Crackers:* Triscuit crackers spread with tunafish salad (tuna, mayonnaise, sweet pickle relish) and shredded carrot. Eat open-faced or top with another Triscuit cracker.
- *Turkey Bagel:* Plain or onion bagel, cream cheese, sliced turkey, lettuce, sliced tomatoes, cucumbers, and sunflower seeds.
- *The Not-Healthy Triple-B Sandwich:* Brie cheese, butter, and bacon layered on any kind of bread you want. This is soooo bad for you but soooo tasty. Eat sparingly lest you clog all your arteries at once.

   More sandwich recipes can be found starting on p. 93.

Favorite Recipes and Basic Ingredients

On the next page is a chart showing some basic ingredients that you may have around your kitchen and a helpful checklist of some of our favorite recipes that use these ingredients. This is very handy when you have a lot of stuff in your pantry but still feel as though "there's nothing to eat in the house!"

   We have left space for you to add your own favorite recipes and ingredients.

Smart Substitutions

When cooking, you can often substitute ingredients or change the amount called for in order to lower the calorie or fat content of your dish, without any noticeable degradation in taste. Some substitutions are based on common sense (less oil in your vinaigrette, or grilling meat instead of pan-frying), but

A PANTRY FULL OF FOOD AND NOT A THING TO EAT?

Basic Ingredients

Basic Ingredients	Fresh Southwest Chicken Salad (p. 136)	Light and Tangy Southwestern Soup (p. 177)	Practically Immediate Baked Potatoes (p. 122)	Bob's Poached Fish on the Grill (p. 75)	Weekend Chili (p. 106)	Festival Pasta Salad (p. 134)	Roasted Fish with Olives (p. 79)	Vegetarian Taco Salad (p. 144)	Orange Chicken Pasta (p. 86)	Zucchini Mushroom Marsala (p. 128)	Greek Rice Florentine (p. 165)	Spicy Spinach Angel Hair (p. 124)
Beans (black, pinto, etc.)	*				*			*				
Bell pepper				*	*	*						
Cheese			*		*			*			*	*
Chicken	*								*			
Cilantro	*	*										
Corn	*	*			*							
Fish				*			*					
Jalapeño pepper								*				*
Lettuce								*				
Mushrooms			*				*		*	*		*
Olives						*	*	*		*		
Onions	*			*	*			*	*	*	*	*
Orange juice									*			
Pasta						*			*	*		*
Potato			*									
Rice											*	
Spinach											*	*
Tomatoes	*	*	*		*						*	
Wine				*						*	*	
Zucchini										*		

it's not always that easy. The trick is knowing when to substitute and when to leave well enough alone! So here we present you with some helpful tips for successful ingredient substitution.

Keep in mind that humans do need a certain amount of fat in our diets to stay healthy. Seeking out foods that are naturally low in fat is a great way to eat, but don't go overboard in avoiding fat. You need it for your health— and it provides much of the flavor and texture (crispness, moistness, creaminess, smoothness) of foods. All things in moderation!

GROUND BEEF

You have probably noticed that ground beef goes by several different names, including sirloin, chuck, and round, but you may not know that they all differ in fat content. Most beef, both at the deli counter and prepackaged, lists the fat percentage prominently on the label. Ground beef that is labeled "sirloin" is generally the healthiest at 10 percent fat or less. "Round" and "chuck" contain 15 percent and 20 percent, respectively, and packages labeled simply "ground beef" with no percentage may contain up to 30 percent fat. For a 4-ounce serving of meat, that's more than 24 grams of fat. And just to provide some perspective on that number, the average American adult should eat about 65 grams of fat or less per day.

If you are used to buying ground chuck or round, consider gradually switching to sirloin. Fat helps keep the meat tender and provides some of the flavor, but as long as your beef contains 7 to 10 percent fat, you should still end up with a very flavorful dish.

You can make the change gradually by mixing equal parts sirloin and your regular ground beef together (yes, by hand—it's squishy but it works). Next time, use more sirloin and less regular beef, until after a few shopping trips you are buying only the sirloin.

If you are cooking beef crumbled in a pan, another way to reduce the calories and fat content is to drain the grease from the skillet both during and after cooking. You can drain by scooping the meat from the pan with a slotted spoon and placing it on paper towels to drain, or simply pour off the fat into an empty metal can, holding the beef back with a slotted spoon. You can even briefly rinse cooked crumbled beef in a colander under hot running water, but we wouldn't recommend this unless you are using the beef in a recipe that has a lot of flavor from other ingredients. If the recipe relies heavily on the beef for flavor, then you've just rinsed away a good portion of that.

If you are making hamburgers, grill them instead of pan-frying, if possible.

That way, the excess fat drips off into the fire (and lends a wonderfully smoky flavor to the burgers) instead of the patties swimming in their own grease.

DAIRY

You have to be very careful when choosing whether or not to switch out dairy ingredients for their lower-fat counterparts. We can't recommend *ever* using fat-free cheese, sour cream, or margarine. Ever. They feel rubbery and plasticky, and taste terrible. You can occasionally get away with reduced-fat versions of these three, but the taste is definitely not the same, especially with the sour cream.

YOGURT

Fat-free plain yogurt is almost always a fine substitute for regular yogurt. Choose organic if you can find it; the taste is unparalleled. Good brands are Stonyfield Farm Organic and Horizon. Katy's favorite is organic lowfat plain yogurt, which has a little extra richness not provided by the fat-free variety. You can find organic yogurt at health food stores and some supermarkets.

For sweetened or flavored yogurt, fat-free is fine, but definitely stay away from any sugar-free variety—yogurt made with artificial sweeteners tastes awful. We recommend avoiding aspartame (a.k.a. Nutrasweet) and saccharin as a rule anyway, so if you're worried about your sugar intake, go for plain yogurt instead and add some sliced fresh fruit and a sprinkle of cinnamon.

MARGARINE VS. BUTTER

Even though margarine has fewer calories and fat grams than butter for the same size portion and is cholesterol free, you're better off sticking with the "real thing." Not only does butter taste richer and fresher, it's healthier because it hasn't been processed and had preservatives and other chemicals added to it. Butter contains only cream and sometimes a little salt.

Margarine, on the other hand, is made from vegetable oil, which goes through a process called hydrogenation in order to get it to stay solid at room temperature. This process creates "trans fatty acids," and recent research has shown that these are linked to increased incidence of coronary heart disease.

If you are a lacto-ovo-vegetarian or are cutting back on cholesterol, or if you don't eat butter for whatever reason, then try to find a margarine that specifically says that it contains no trans fatty acids. Smart Balance is one such brand. We have chosen to use butter instead of margarine in all our recipes in this book, but in most cases you can substitute margarine if you want to.

SOUR CREAM

Avoid fat-free sour cream. It tastes vaguely sweet and sort of gritty and chalky. Reduced-fat sour cream is fine, although the consistency is thinner than regular sour cream, so if you're cooking with it, you should reduce the other liquids in the recipe a little. The best sour cream we've found is Borden brand "all natural" sour cream, meaning that it contains no preservatives or chemicals whatsoever.

MILK

If you drink a lot of milk, then you probably already have a preferred favorite type. Katy drinks either skim or 1 percent most of the time, although her husband Doc says that skim is just like opaque water, so why bother? Well, it's a lot lower in fat, for one thing. If you want to switch to a lower-fat milk, do it gradually. Go from whole to 2 percent to 1 percent to ½ percent (if available) to skim. We find that 1 percent milk, however, has the best balance of flavor and healthiness. It's generally OK to use skim or lowfat milk in cooking where regular milk is called for, though the final result may be somewhat less rich.

CHEESE

Some cheese is naturally low in fat—look for varieties such as Parmesan or Romano. The general rule of thumb is: the harder the cheese, the lower the fat content, and (often) the stronger the flavor. You don't need to use as much of a stronger-flavored cheese to achieve the same results, and so this also helps cut down on fat.

ICE CREAM

Lower-fat versions of regular ice cream are often an acceptable substitutes for regular, although, like most other dairy products, the taste is not quite the same. The only fat-free ice cream we like is not ice cream at all—it's soft-serve frozen yogurt. Frozen yogurt is quite delicious, be it fat-free or merely lowfat, but beware the high-calorie toppings that tantalize you from behind the counter at the yogurt shop. And fat-free does not mean calorie-free! Sorbet and sherbet, which are naturally low in fat, are other good alternatives to ice cream when you are having a frozen-dessert craving.

REFRIED BEANS

Canned refried beans never taste quite like those that Mexican restaurants serve, usually because the freshly made variety is cooked with liberal amounts of lard or vegetable oil. Canned beans can be dressed up with spices like cumin, oregano, and chili powder to improve the taste, and the fat-free type can be used interchangeably with regular or vegetarian types with practically no discernible difference in taste.

FAT-FREE SNACKS (COOKIES AND CRACKERS)

Prepackaged "fat-free" processed snack foods—most notably those in green boxes which subconsciously make you think that the contents are good for you—are notoriously deceptive. Have you ever checked out the nutrition label side by side with a comparable "regular" snack? You may be surprised at what you'll find. Sometimes the only way to make something fat-free is to boost the sugar content through the roof, so the calorie count of that fat-free snack is nearly as high as the regular version. And when it comes right down to it, your total calorie intake matters more than the fat grams.

OLESTRA

You may have heard of new snack products made with Olestra, an oil substitute approved by the FDA for use in savory snack foods. Olestra works because it isn't absorbed by your body when you eat it—its molecules are larger than those of ordinary fats and don't get digested. After a somewhat hesitant personal research experiment, Katy concluded that Olestra-fried chips taste almost exactly like regular chips—enough to fool her if she didn't know which ones she was eating. However, there is a lot of controversy surrounding the use of Olestra. One known side effect is the loss of fat-soluble vitamins from your body—vitamins A, D, E, and K. The FDA requires that products that use Olestra be vitamin-fortified for this reason. The jury is still out on this issue.

MACARONI AND CHEESE

Many of us still love this old standby in the blue box well into adulthood. Most boxed macaroni and cheese dinners have instructions for a lower-calorie version printed on the box. Making it the regular way uses an entire half stick of butter! And that box is supposed to serve four, but let's not kid ourselves—most of us can stretch that to maybe two servings, no more. That's a whole lot of butter per person. Follow the low-fat instructions instead, which call for a mere 2 tablespoons of butter. If you like, mix in a teaspoon or so of Tabasco sauce or spicy brown mustard to add a tangy kick. Arushi recommends adding lots of your favorite salsa. You can gradually reduce the amount of butter in your mac 'n' cheese if you're used to using the half-stick. Use less each time and you might be surprised at how little you notice the difference.

VINAIGRETTE DRESSING

Many vinaigrette recipes call for four times more oil than vinegar. You can get away with *a lot* less oil—the vinegar is what gives the dressing its flavor, while the oil mainly serves to spread the dressing around and coat the salad evenly. Just decrease the amount of oil to be equal to or less than the amount of vinegar, and you'll do fine. You'll also end up using a lot less dressing this way.

FRUIT PULP

Fruit pulp is meant to be a substitute for some or all of the fat in baked goods. It's exactly what it says—mashed-up fruit. It provides some of the moisture in baked goods, which is usually the job of the butter or oil. However, you tend to end up with a denser, drier product. Follow the instructions on the label if you do use it. Fruit pulp can be found in the baking section of most supermarkets.

TOMATO-BASED PASTA SAUCE

We all know that Alfredo sauce, deliciously creamy and cheesy and well worth the occasional indulgence, is very high in fat and calories. But did you know that tomato-based pasta sauces may not be as low-fat as you think? Check the nutrition label on bottled sauces if you buy these—some can contain as much as 50 percent of their calories from fat (thought it's usually in the form of olive oil, which is actually fairly good for you as far as fats go). Katy rarely uses bottled pasta sauce, but when she does she prefers the taste of sauce made with little or no oil—the flavors are stronger and fresher. Of course, homemade sauces are best (such as Katy's Garlic Mushroom Red Sauce, p. 117, which can easily be frozen in single-serving sizes for later use), but realistically it's a good idea to keep a jar of sauce on hand for those nights that you just don't have the energy to cook from scratch.

REDUCING THE AMOUNT OF BUTTER YOU USE AS A SPREAD

OK, this may sound like torture, but it does work. To break yourself of the habit of using a lot of butter on toast, bagels, English muffins, or rolls, try this easy trick: Eat them dry for a few weeks. No, really! Eat dry toast or dry bagels, get used to the taste . . . and then let yourself use a tiny amount of butter. It will taste like heaven, your mouth will thank you for bringing back that wonderful creamy taste and texture, and you'll use a lot less than you did before. Remember, butter contains 11 grams of fat per tablespoon, which is approximately one-sixth of your recommended daily allowance of fat.

Healthy Snacking

While it's always a great idea to keep healthy snacks on hand, such as baby carrots and celery sticks, fruit slices, pretzels and saltines, sometimes you just *have to* satisfy a craving for something sweet or something salty. It's okay to buy your favorite junk foods on occasion, but if you have a tendency to go through a quart of ice cream or a bag of chips in under a week, like we do, then these tips might help:

• Never eat directly from a big bag of chips! (This applies to cookies and crackers, too.) It's nearly impossible to judge exactly how much you've eaten, and you'll almost always underestimate the actual quantity you've consumed. While single-serving packages of these snacks are convenient, it's a lot more economical to buy the regular-size bag. A trick for this is to put just a handful or two of chips into sandwich-size plastic zipper bags for sack lunches, or put a handful directly on your plate and then put the big bag back in the pantry. This is a pretty easy way to exercise portion control.

• Don't eat junk food in front of the TV. Arushi recommends munching on celery sticks or carrots instead. (Yes, she actually does this). They can satisfy your oral cravings, and many of us eat in front of the TV not because we are actually hungry, but simply because we are used to snacking there.

• With ice cream, don't eat directly from the carton! (Even if it's just a pint.) Get a small bowl and put one or two kid-size scoops into that. Ice cream in a small bowl will look a lot more satisfying than the same amount in a large bowl. And you can always tell yourself that if you really *must* have more when you are finished with the first bowl, then you can go get more. That small amount can often be enough to satisfy your craving, though.

• With soft drinks, although it's often more economical to buy a 2-liter bottle, we always feel compelled to finish it off before it goes flat. Twelve-ounce cans (or the old-fashioned 8-ounce glass bottles) really help with portion control, and often the larger packages (24 cans) are sale-priced so that they're no more expensive per ounce than the larger bottles.

Packing Lunchboxes

If you take your lunch to work with you, it's easy to fall into the rut of taking the same one or two things day in and day out. Sandwich, frozen microwaveable meal, sandwich, frozen meal. How do you keep your lunches interesting, and at the same time, easy to prepare? One way is to take leftovers with you, and even possibly transforming them into a different meal. Try packing a leftover grilled chicken breast along with a container of chopped lettuce, shredded carrot, and sliced cucumber, plus a little leftover plain pasta and a container of salad dressing. Instant chicken salad! You can also make a dish specifically for lunches, such as a batch of Festival Pasta Salad, p. 134, and take it several days during the week. Here are some other options:

Making Sandwiches Better

Sandwiches made several hours in advance tend to become a bit soggy by the time you get around to eating them. Remember back in school, when sandwiches sat in your locker all morning? To avoid this, pack the ingredients separately and construct your sandwich when it's time to eat it. It is a bit more work this way but it sure beats a soggy sandwich.

You can buy disposable 2-ounce plastic portion cups (the kind restaurants fill with sauces to go) from warehouse food clubs or some supermarkets. These are terrific for holding small amounts of mayonnaise, mustard, pickle chips, sliced vegetables, or any number of snacks such as nuts, olives, or raisins. Sandwich-size or snack-size plastic zipper bags can be used for bread, cheeses, lettuce, and meats. And we always keep leftover condiment packets from restaurants; they work great for this purpose.

For a change of pace, make your sandwich on a bagel instead of bread, or rolled up inside a tortilla. Something as simple as heating up the sandwich can instantly make it new and interesting. Arushi likes to take sandwich ingredients and put them in an omelet instead of using bread. For more great sandwich ideas, see the Mix-and-Match Sandwich Chart, p. 24.

Things that go great with sandwiches include chips, pretzels, crackers, Baked French Fries (p. 159), raisins, a piece of fruit, carrot or celery sticks, cubed cheese, a small salad, or a small bowl of soup.

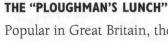

THE "PLOUGHMAN'S LUNCH"

Popular in Great Britain, the Ploughman's Lunch is a box lunch often served at pubs alongside pints of ale. Easily prepared ahead of time, it is perfect for a quick snack or meal. It generally consists of a slab of cheese, bread, Branston Pickle (a sweet relish made from assorted vegetables) and any number of vegetables like tomatoes, lettuce, or coleslaw.

Branston Pickle is not easy to find in the United States, so you could substitute small sweet pickles or even dill, if you prefer. But you can include anything you like in your Ploughman's Lunch. It's a terrific way to use leftovers. Just remember: small bits of a lot of different things! Those little portion cups are great for this purpose, too.

Some foods you can include in your Ploughman's Lunch:

- Crackers
- Chunks of hearty bread
- Pita bread, torn in pieces
- Small container of dip or hummus
- Cheese (cubed or sliced)
- Leftover grilled chicken, pepperoni slices, or other meats
- Small sweet or dill pickles
- A piece of fruit, sliced or cut into chunks
- Grapes
- Baby carrots
- Celery sticks
- Nuts
- Olives
- Raisins, dried apricot, or other dried fruit
- Cookies
- M&Ms

Basic Recipes

You need to know a few very basic recipes to be successful in the kitchen. Once you can do these, you are prepared to make just about anything. Following these recipes is a handy list that will help clear up some of the mysteries surrounding food preparation techniques.

RICE

A rice steamer is a very handy gadget to have; it can be used for a lot more than just rice. You can also cook rice in a pot on the stove. Use twice as much water as you do rice. Put the water and rice in the pot together with a dash of salt, stir briefly, and then set on the stove on high. Let it come to a boil. Reduce the heat to medium-low, cover the pot, and let the rice simmer until it is cooked through and all the water is absorbed. Don't stir the rice or lift the lid while it's cooking. This usually takes about 20 minutes for one cup of white rice. When done, remove from the heat and fluff with a fork. White rice generally yields about three times what you started with—so one cup of raw rice gives you three cups cooked.

Seasonings can be added to the rice and water to lend a nice flavor. Chicken or vegetable bouillon is a good one, or try using chicken broth instead of water. Lemon juice and fresh or dried herbs work well, too, as does Lipton Onion Soup Mix.

A time saving hint: Some people opt to save the cooking time on rice by using "instant" varieties such as Minute Rice, which can be prepared in about 5 minutes. Unfortunately, this precooked, dried, and reconstituted rice tastes starchy and mealy. A perfectly acceptable way to save time is to buy a take-out container of freshly steamed rice from an Asian restaurant.

BAKED POTATOES

Potatoes can be cooked either in the microwave or (ideally) the oven. To microwave them, scrub them under the faucet, pat dry, poke a few holes in the skins, wrap in waxed paper, and microwave for approximately 6 to 8 minutes for one potato or 8 to 10 minutes for two. Use russet or Idaho baking potatoes for best results.

To oven-bake potatoes, give yourself at least one hour's baking time. Scrub the potatoes under the faucet, pat dry, and poke a few holes in the skins. Insert a metal skewer all the way through the potato the long way. Bake in a 375° oven for 45 minutes to an hour for two potatoes, an hour to an hour and 15 minutes for four. The metal skewer heats up and helps cook the potato from the inside. You can rub the skins with some olive oil before you bake them, if you like.

MASHED POTATOES

Mashed potatoes are a true American comfort food. They are a holiday dinner standard as well as an everyday meal tradition. And you can buy instant mashed potato flakes to reconstitute with water, but they just don't taste the same as what Mom used to make. The good news is, it is very easy to make your own mashed potatoes.

Take two russet or Idaho baking potatoes, rinse under the faucet, and peel with a vegetable peeler. Cut the potatoes into chunks about 1-inch square. Get a large pot of water boiling, and put in the potatoes. Boil for about 10 minutes, or until the potatoes are soft and cooked through. Drain the water, and mash the potatoes slightly with a potato masher or a fork. Add any or all of the following: butter, milk, cream, chicken or vegetable broth, sour cream, garlic, Parmesan cheese. Mash again, just until mixed. If you overmix, the potatoes will be dense instead of light and fluffy. Add salt and pepper to taste. Serve with butter or gravy, if desired.

HARD BOILED EGGS

Place eggs (up to four) in the bottom of a medium saucepan. Add water so the eggs are covered by at least one inch of water. Bring the pot to a boil. Once it has started boiling, turn off the heat, cover the pot, and let the eggs sit for 15 minutes. Drain the water and add cold water to the pan along with a few ice cubes. Let the eggs sit in the cold water for about 2 minutes. To remove the shell, gently tap it all over on the countertop to crack it, and then gently peel. Holding the egg under running water often helps get the shell off.

SCRAMBLED EGGS

With a fork or whisk, beat 1 egg with 1 tablespoon of milk and salt and pepper to taste. (For 2 eggs, use 2 tablespoons of milk, and so on.) In a skillet heat 1 teaspoon of butter over medium heat. Pour in the eggs. As the eggs begin to set, stir slightly with a wooden spoon to break up. As they set more and more, give them a few gentle stirs, just to make sure all the egg gets cooked. The egg is done when there is no more liquid egg visible.

MAKING OMELETS

Omelets are great for any meal, not just breakfast. In the morning, they can be made with ham and cheese, green peppers, and onions. For dinner, they can be filled with any leftovers or vegetables, even rice. If you think of an omelet as another type of sandwich that uses eggs instead of bread, you can get really creative.

For a single omelet, briefly whisk two eggs until slightly frothy. Heat a bit of vegetable oil in a nonstick skillet on medium-high heat. Once the oil is warm, turn the heat down to medium. Add the eggs. Stir frequently until the eggs look like they are about to scramble, then stop and let the omelet set. Be patient, since this may take about 5 minutes, which feels like an eternity when you are watching an omelet. As it sets, sprinkle your favorite fillings on one half of the omelet. When it's set, fold the naked half over and scoot the omelet out of the pan onto a serving plate.

BASIC FRUIT SALAD

A fruit salad makes a fast, elegant, and healthy dessert or side dish, bringing freshness and brightness to any meal. A basic fruit salad uses whatever fruits are in season, in whatever proportions you like. It can be a mixture of berries and melons in summer or a fruit and cheese plate in winter. We recently made a salad from strawberries and papayas simply because that was what was sitting in the refrigerator.

Use the fruits you think are the prettiest and tastiest, and cut them into bite-size pieces. You can add a little sugar or honey if you want some added sweetness, but the fruits are usually sweet enough by themselves. Stir to blend, and serve chilled or at room temperature.

Remember that not all fruits are created equal. Pears and apples turn brown soon after they are cut, so they should be eaten quickly or paired with an acidic fruit that prevents browning, like pineapple, grapefruit, or even a squirt of lemon juice.

For a festive look, spoon the fruit salad into parfait glasses and top with a spoonful of cream (whipped or unwhipped) or vanilla ice cream and a dash of cinnamon. Or, cut apples or pears and place them along with a block of cheese on a small cutting board and serve.

BAKED CHICKEN BREASTS

Chicken breasts can be prepared in a myriad of ways, including boiling (great for making shredded chicken), grilling, batter-frying, and sautéing. But probably the quickest, most hassle-free way to cook chicken is to bake it in the oven.

Chicken can be preseasoned with any type of marinade or spice that you like. There is a terrific recipe on p. 99 for Lemon Herb Chicken. Often salt and pepper is all you need, especially if you have prepared a sauce to go with the chicken.

"Brining" a chicken breast before grilling or baking helps keep it very tender, juicy, and flavorful. Soak the chicken for about 30 minutes in a mixture of water, salt, and sugar—about 2 tablespoons salt and 1 tablespoon sugar for every cup of water. Add other marinade ingredients such as soy sauce to the brine if you like. Drain off the brine, and grill or bake as normal.

For a basic baked chicken breast, preheat the oven to 400°. Place the chicken breast on a lightly oiled baking sheet. Drizzle with a teaspoon or two of olive oil, and sprinkle with salt and pepper. Bake for 25 minutes, or until the chicken is cooked through and its juices run clear.

You can use skinless chicken breasts, but we prefer to use breasts with

the skin on, and remove it after cooking. It helps keep the chicken moist and flavorful as it cooks and, if removed later, adds very little extra fat.

PASTA

Different types of pasta have different cooking times. The thicker or larger the pasta shape, the longer it needs to cook. Your recipe or the pasta package will tell you how long your particular type needs to cook.

In general, though, you should bring a large pot of water to a boil over high heat. Add a dash of salt to the water. Some people like to add a few teaspoons of oil to the water, though this is not necessary. Both the salt and the oil can help prevent the water from boiling over. Once the water is boiling vigorously, add the pasta. For long straight pasta such as spaghetti that won't completely fit in the pot at once, let the part that is in the water soften a bit, then push the rest of it down until it is all immersed. Let the pasta boil, uncovered, for as long as directed. Leaving a wooden spoon parked across the top of the pot or in the water itself can also help prevent boil-overs.

You should cook pasta until it is al dente, or tender but still somewhat firm to the bite. Test it by actually tasting a piece. It should not be at all crunchy, but yet somewhat firm. Once cooked, drain pasta in a large colander or strainer (metal mesh ones work grea). Do not rinse the pasta! Rinsing washes away surface starch, which is what helps sauces to stick to the pasta. You may add a little olive oil if you like, to prevent the pasta from sticking together.

SAUTÉED VEGETABLES

It is quite easy to sauté vegetables as a side dish or as a stir-fry meal; just remember that the softer the vegetable, the shorter the cooking time. For instance, carrots take longer to cook than mushrooms. Cut your vegetables into bite-size pieces. Put a little butter or olive oil in a skillet over medium-high heat. When hot, add garlic and/or onion if you wish, and sauté for a few minutes until the onion is translucent and golden. Add any other vegetables that you like, and stir frequently until the vegetables are softened to your liking. Add salt, pepper, and any other spices. You can also add a sauce or marinade at this time, and continue cooking until the sauce is bubbly.

GRAVY

We all know that you can buy pre-made gravy in a jar or frozen, or make it from a packet mix. But Katy's mom has a quick and easy method for making gravy after cooking a roast or a turkey. And you can even freeze pan drippings for making the gravy at a later time.

With a spoon, carefully spoon off most of the fat and oil floating on top of the pan drippings, and discard. Pour the remaining juices into a skillet, being sure to scrape up and include any browned bits from the bottom of the pan, and set it on the stove over medium-high heat. Meanwhile, in a jar with a tight-fitting lid, shake together 1 cup water and ½ cup flour. Make sure it's completely smooth and blended with no lumps.

When the pan drippings come to a boil, start whisking them with one hand and slowly pour the flour mixture into the pan with the other. It's very important to do this slowly and whisk constantly. The gravy will quickly thicken. You may not need to use all the flour mixture. Once the gravy is thick, season to taste with salt and pepper. If the gravy needs some extra flavor, stir in a package of Lipton Onion Soup Mix.

SALAD DRESSING

Many vinaigrette dressings call for a lot more oil than they do vinegar, but we prefer to use a higher percentage of vinegar to strengthen the flavor and cut down on the fat. The dressing gets its flavor from the vinegar and spices; the oil serves mainly to spread the dressing around and coat the lettuce leaves. A good ratio of oil to vinegar is 50/50.

Make the vinaigrette with olive or vegetable oil, vinegar, salt, pepper, and any spices you like: we love using basil, oregano, and thyme. Experiment with different kinds of vinegar, such as balsamic, red wine, or tarragon. You can also add a spoonful of spicy mustard, a squirt of lemon juice, or a dash of sugar. You can blend the dressing in the blender, to completely incorporate the oil and vinegar, or just stir with a spoon or shake up the jar before pouring.

SIMPLE CHEESE QUESADILLAS

This has got to be the easiest snack on the planet. Take a large flour tortilla, sprinkle it with your favorite cheese, add salt and pepper, and fold it in half. Spray a skillet with vegetable oil spray and heat it over medium-high heat. Cook the quesadilla for just a minute or two on both sides, until the cheese begins to melt and browned spots appear.

Pop it in the oven for a few minutes, if you have the time, to melt the cheese even further.

You can also add anything you like to the quesadilla: onions, prosciutto, asparagus, sun-dried tomatoes, mushrooms, cooked chicken breast slices, spices. Be creative!

WHIPPED CREAM

This is a really tough job if you don't have an electric mixer. It can be done by hand with a wire whisk, but you'll get a real workout doing it. Combine 2 cups of whipping (heavy) cream with a teaspoon each of sugar and vanilla extract. Beat on high speed until stiff peaks form in the cream (which means that when you dip a spoon in the cream and pull it up, the little peak will retain its shape without softening). You can add more sugar if you like a sweeter whipped cream, but the mixing time will increase slightly. Whipped cream is also great with a little cinnamon added.

Techniques

DEVEINING SHRIMP

Fresh shrimp usually need to have the "vein," or intestine, removed before cooking. You will need a paring knife and cold running water. First, remove the legs, shell, and tail from the shrimp by gently pulling them off under running water. Then make a ⅛″ to ¼″ slit all the way down the center of the back of the shrimp. With the tip of the knife or your fingers, pull out the dark vein. The shrimp is then ready for cooking.

DRAINING FAT FROM COOKED MEAT

You can drain the grease from cooked ground beef or turkey by scooping the meat from the pan with a slotted spoon and placing it on paper towels to drain, or simply pouring off the fat into an empty metal can, holding the meat back with a slotted spoon.

CHECKING MEAT FOR DONENESS

Sometimes meat looks done on the outside, but how do you tell whether it's cooked all the way through? Simple: you look inside.

Check fish by cutting open the fillet at the thickest part and making sure it is opaque all the way through. Check chicken or pork by cutting open at the thickest part and making sure it is no longer pink at the center, and that the juices run clear. Steak should be checked the same way—well done means no pink at the center.

CHOPPING OR SLICING AN ONION

Figuring out how to cut an onion can be confusing, because of the way onions are constructed. Do you cut across? Down? Did you mean to make rings but cut the wrong way and sliced them all in half? Here are some easy instructions for slicing, chopping, and making rings out of an onion.

Cut a thin slice from both the root end and the top of the onion. Peel off the papery skin. Sometimes the outer layer of onion will come with it; this is OK. All of the following instructions begin with the onion flat side down on a cutting board.

Slicing into strips: Slice vertically down through the onion, cutting it in half. Put each half flat side down on the cutting board, and make crosswise cuts all the way across each half.

Chopping: Slice vertically down through the onion, cutting it in half. Put each half flat side down on the cutting board, and make lengthwise cuts all the way across each half, then crosswise cuts, to form little diced onion bits.

Slicing into rings: Turn the onion onto a rounded side, and cut vertically downward into slices, however thick you like. Separate into rings.

PEELING AND MINCING GARLIC

The simplest way to mince garlic is to lay the unpeeled clove on a cutting board and, using the heel of your hand, gently squash it under the flat of a large knife blade. The papery skin should be easily removable, and you can slice the garlic lengthwise and then crosswise with the knife, making little dice.

Some people prefer to use a garlic press, where you squeeze the handle and the mashed garlic comes out the little holes, but this pretty much pulverizes the garlic into a big squishy chunk. Plus, you waste almost half the clove because not all the garlic comes out of the holes.

We have discovered a terrific tool for peeling garlic that you can get at kitchen supply stores. It's a simple flexible rubber tube into which you place the garlic, press and roll gently against the counter, and the skins come off like magic. Or you can just put on clean rubber kitchen gloves and roll the garlic in your palms. This works great when you don't actually want to break the garlic clove.

MAKING CITRUS ZEST

Zest simply refers to the top layer of a citrus fruit's rind. This colored part is the part that has the lemon, lime, or orange flavor; the white "pith" underneath is quite bitter. You can grate zest by using either the fine holes of a cheese grater or a citrus-zesting tool, which looks like a little handle with tiny sharp-edged rings on the end.

Use the zesting tool by digging the sharp rings slightly into the peel, then gently pulling the tool toward you, grating the peel off in long strips. Take care not to grate any of the white pith. If the zest strips are too long, you can chop them up with a knife.

Zesting with a cheese grater tends to produce shorter zest strips. Don't use the ragged-edged holes on a box-style grater; you will simply end up with a mushy mess of purée. In fact, we can't figure out what you are actually supposed to use those ragged holes for. Use the small clean-edged holes instead.

BAKING COOKIES

When baking cookies, you should generally put about 12 cookies on each standard-size baking sheet, in three rows of four. You need a lot of space between cookies because they tend to spread out as they bake, especially the softer varieties like chocolate chip or snickerdoodles. Firmer cookies such as gingersnaps spread less, but still need one to two inches between cookies.

Follow your recipe's instructions as to whether to use a greased or an ungreased baking sheet. Baking sheets should be light in color, if possible, because darker ones will burn the bottoms of the cookies faster. Nonstick sheets are always the best option, and if you can afford to spring for sturdy high-quality professional ones, you won't regret it.

If you are going for chewier cookies, bake them for the least amount of time indicated by your recipe—or sometimes a minute or two less. They should be firm around the edges and still soft in the center. They need to "set" on the baking sheet for several minutes after you remove them from the oven. If you try to take them off the baking sheet too soon, they will fall apart. Crisper cookies should be cooked for the longest amount of time indicated by your recipe. However, don't cook them long enough to let them burn on the bottom.

SLICING MEAT

Meats such as chicken, pork, and steak are a lot easier to cut into slices or pieces when they are partially frozen. Always defrost meat in the refrigerator, and never on the counter. If you buy it fresh, put it in the freezer for an hour or so. When the meat is frozen but still somewhat flexible, take it out and slice away. You will find that you have a lot more control over the thinness and the shape of your slices.

CRUSHING CRUMBS

To make crumbs for coating vegetables or meat (such as Flattened Oven-Fried Chicken, p. 91) or for pie crusts (like Dad's Lemon Meringue Pie,

p. 184), put your crackers or cookies into a large zip-top plastic bag, remove most of the air, and seal. Use your hands, a rolling pin, or a soup can from your pantry to roll and crush until you are left with fine crumbs.

Alternately, you can use a food processor or blender to make crumbs. Just be sure to have the lid on tightly, because otherwise the crumbs will fly all over your kitchen and you'll be finding them for weeks. Trust us on this one!

SCOOPING OUT AN AVOCADO

Buy avocados that are large, very green in color, and slightly soft to the touch. Too soft, and they are usually rotten; too firm, and they are hard as rocks. Cut the avocado in half lengthwise, slicing around the pit. Remove the pit and discard. With a spoon, gently scoop the smooth green "meat" out of the avocado skins. Discard the skins.

SHREDDING LETTUCE OR CABBAGE

Unless you plan to serve shredded lettuce or cabbage immediately, don't use a metal knife because it will cause the edges of the greens to quickly turn brown. Sharp plastic knives specifically for cutting lettuce are available at kitchen supply stores.

If you do plan to use the greens right away, you can shred them with either a food processor or a knife. A food processor works best on cabbage and heads of lettuce that are "tight," such as iceberg. Cut the head in half (removing the tough core) and then into quarters or smaller sections. Feed each section into the food processor fitted with a slicer blade.

To use a knife, cut the head of lettuce in half (removing the tough core), and place each half flat side down on a cutting board. With a large knife such as a chef's knife or a plastic lettuce knife, make thin lengthwise slices. If the shreds are too long, you can cut them in half crosswise. This also works for "looser" heads of lettuce like Romaine or bunches of spinach. Just keep the bunch packed tightly together with your hand, and use the knife to make thin slices.

SEEDING A TOMATO

It's perfectly OK to eat the seeds of a fresh tomato, but some people do prefer to remove both the seeds and the gelatinous material surrounding them. To do this, cut the tomato in half horizontally. With your clean fingers or a small spoon, scoop out the seeds and gel, and rinse the tomato half under cool running water to remove any remaining seeds. Then you can cut it into slices or chop it, according to your needs.

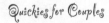

PEELING A TOMATO

It's not very often that you need to peel a tomato, but some recipes do call for it. Luckily, it's quite easy to do. Get a pot of water boiling on the stove. With a sharp knife, cut a shallow X into the skin of each tomato. Drop the tomatoes into the boiling water, and boil for about 30 to 40 seconds. Use a slotted spoon to removed the tomatoes, and immediately drop them into a bowl of ice water to stop the cooking process. The skins should be very easy to slip off.

PEELING ORANGES

A cool trick to get an orange to loosen inside of its peel is to drop it into boiling water for about a minute, remove it with a slotted spoon, and drop it into a bowl of ice water. This seems to work great for getting the peel to come off the orange easily.

To peel it, cut an X into one end of the orange with a small knife. Cut all the way through the peel but not too far into the orange. Using your thumbs, pull back the rind from the X and tear away the peel.

CLEANING AND TRIMMING MUSHROOMS

There is disagreement among chefs over whether you should ever rinse mushrooms directly under running water. Conventional wisdom says to use only a damp paper towel to wipe them off, but we've always found it faster and easier to rinse mushrooms under water, and it seems to work perfectly well. Either way, you need to get the dirt off. If you rinse them under water, quickly pat them dry with a paper towel lest they become too waterlogged, as they are somewhat absorbent.

Once cleaned, trim about ½ inch off of the stem, and cut away any brown spots.

DESTEMMING STRAWBERRIES

Special strawberry destemming tools are available, but you can do just as good a job with a simple vegetable peeler. Rinse the strawberries under cool running water (do this just before serving, lest they become mushy from sitting too long). Pull off the green leaves from the end, and use the tip of the vegetable peeler to cut down into the top of the strawberry in a circle, removing the core.

STORING AND SERVING WINE

There is not much mystery about the average wine. Don't let the fancy names fool you: all wine is basically grape juice for adults. Wines come in all price ranges and from all over the planet. Try to keep at least one red and one white variety on hand, and don't worry about whether it's a "good" wine or not. If you like it, that's all that matters.

Store wine bottles on their sides, with the mouth of the bottle tilted slightly downward. Once opened, a bottle will keep for about a week. After that, the wine may not taste right for drinking, but it's still fine for cooking.

White wines are typically served chilled, so keep them in the refrigerator. They are usually paired with lighter meals, such as fish, poultry, salads, and pastas.

Red wines are generally paired with richer, heavier foods and with red meats. They also go surprisingly well with spicy cuisines like Indian or Thai food. Red wines are usually served at room temperature, and Arushi recommends letting them "breathe" for 30 minutes before serving.

Appetizers

Hot Crab Dip

Mom suggests adding some shredded Parmesan cheese, spreading the mixture on toasted English muffins, and broiling until browned and crispy.

4	ounces cream cheese
½	cup mayonnaise
1	6-ounce can crab meat, drained
¼	cup minced onion
1	tablespoon lemon juice
¼	teaspoon Tabasco sauce
	Salt and pepper to taste

- Preheat the oven to 350°F.

- In a small bowl beat the cream cheese until smooth using an electric mixer or wooden spoon. Add the mayonnaise, crab, onion, lemon juice, and Tabasco sauce, and stir until blended. Season to taste with salt and pepper.

- Using a spatula, spoon the mixture into a small oven-safe baking dish. Bake, uncovered, for 30 minutes or until bubbly.

- Serve hot.

Equipment
Electric mixer
Small bowl
Small oven-safe baking
dish

Servings
4 to 8

Serving Suggestions
- Crackers
- Vegetable sticks

Preparation Time
10 minutes

Total Time
40 minutes

Italian Pesto Pasta Slices

The first time we made this for a party, all our friends asked for the recipe! The filling can also be stuffed into cooked manicotti shells and sliced. Egg roll wrappers can be found at Asian food markets or in the refrigerated or produce section of most supermarkets.

Equipment
Large pot
Medium bowl

Servings
3 to 4

Preparation Time
20 minutes

Total Time
25 minutes

½	cup orzo or other tiny pasta
¼	cup pesto
2	teaspoons balsamic vinegar
2	tablespoons chives or green onions, minced
¼	cup ricotta cheese
¼	cup oil-packed sun-dried tomatoes, drained and chopped finely
¼	cup Kalamata olives, chopped finely
½	teaspoon salt
¼	teaspoon pepper
3	8-inch-square egg roll wrappers
	Parsley for garnish
	Whole Kalamata olives for garnish

- In a large pot of boiling salted water cook the orzo until tender but still firm to bite. Orzo cooks fast, so taste it every minute or so until it is done. Drain well, but do not rinse.

- In a medium bowl mix the cooked orzo with the pesto, vinegar, chives, ricotta cheese, sun-dried tomatoes, olives, and salt and pepper to taste. Let cool in the refrigerator.

- In a large pot of boiling salted water cook the egg roll wrappers for 15 to 20 seconds, or until softened. (Cooking them longer increases the chances that they will rip.) Rinse and drain the wrappers, being careful not to tear them.

- Lay one cooked wrapper flat on a cutting board. Soak up any excess water with a paper towel, making sure the wrapper is drained fully. Spread a third of the filling on each wrapper, leaving ½-inch space at the far edge.

Tightly roll up the wrapper starting from the edge near you. Seal the edge, using a little water to moisten if necessary.

- Cut each roll into six or eight slices and arrange flat on a serving platter. Garnish with parsley and Kalamata olives. (You can also wrap the rolls tightly in plastic wrap before slicing and refrigerate for up to two days.)

Serve meals in serving bowls, not straight out of the skillet.

Send the kids away for the evening.

Galveston Shrimp Cocktail

The cocktail sauce from this recipe is great not only with boiled shrimp, but also with fried shrimp or fish.

Shrimp:

½	pound medium shrimp
1	12-ounce can beer
1	small onion, sliced
1	clove garlic, minced
1	bay leaf
2	peppercorns
½	teaspoon salt
1	teaspoon seafood seasoning
1	lemon, quartered

Cocktail sauce:

½	cup ketchup
1	tablespoon prepared horseradish
1	teaspoon lemon juice
	Salt and pepper to taste

Equipment
Medium bowl
Medium saucepan

Servings
2 to 4

Serving Suggestions
Cocktail sauce

Preparation Time
10 minutes

Total Time
25 minutes

- Rinse the shrimp, remove the shells, and devein. (To save time, you can ask your butcher to shell and devein the shrimp for you.) Place the shrimp in a bowl and set aside.

- In a medium saucepan simmer the beer, onion, garlic, bay leaf, peppercorns, salt, seafood seasoning, and 2 lemon quarters on medium-high heat, covered, for 10 minutes.

- Turn off the heat but leave the saucepan on the stove. Add the shrimp, cover, and let cook for 4 to 5 minutes, or until the shrimp are opaque and cooked through.

- Meanwhile, make the cocktail sauce. In a small bowl blend the ketchup, horseradish, and lemon juice. Season to taste with salt and pepper.

- Drain the shrimp; serve with extra lemon quarters and cocktail sauce.

Leslie and Bruce's 7-Layer Dip

The guac in this recipe has a little added kick, but you can substitute Speedy Guacamole, p. 59, if you like. Feel free to change the amounts of ingredients in any of the layers to suit your taste.

2	medium-size ripe avocados
1/4	cup minced white onions
1	fresh jalapeño pepper, minced
1/4	cup chopped cilantro
1/4	cup fresh lime juice
	Salt and pepper to taste
1	15-ounce can refried black beans (or regular)
8	ounces sour cream
8	ounces Colby-Jack or Cheddar cheese, grated (about 2 cups)
1	4-ounce can sliced black olives
2	cups shredded iceberg lettuce
1	cup diced tomatoes
	Tortilla chips
	Salsa (try Katy's Hot Salsa, p. 157)

- Cut the avocados in half and remove the pits. With a spoon, scoop the meat of the avocado out of the skin and place it in a medium bowl. Mash the avocado with a fork to desired consistency. Add the onions, jalapeño pepper, cilantro, lime juice, and salt and pepper to taste. Stir the guacamole mixture gently until it is well blended.

- In an 8-inch square glass baking dish (or any other flat-bottomed serving dish you have on hand), spread the ingredients in layers in this order: refried beans, guacamole, sour cream, grated cheese, black olives, lettuce, and tomatoes.

- Serve with tortilla chips and salsa.

Equipment
Medium bowl
8-inch square glass baking dish

Servings
8

Serving Suggestions
- Frozen margaritas
- Mexican beer

Preparation Time
15 minutes

Total Time
15 minutes

Parmesan Twists

These are incredibly addictive. They work great as party appetizers (prepare to make several recipes' worth!) or served alongside an Italian meal. Using fresh Parmesan cheese rather than the grated kind found in shaker cans makes all the difference.

Equipment
Large bowl
Electric mixer
Rolling pin
Baking sheet
Small bowl
Pastry brush
Wire cooling rack

Servings
8

Preparation Time
25 minutes

Total Time
40 minutes

$\frac{1}{4}$ cup butter, softened
1 cup freshly grated Parmesan cheese (prepackaged is fine)
$\frac{1}{2}$ cup sour cream
1 cup flour
$\frac{1}{2}$ teaspoon Italian seasoning (or use thyme, basil, or oregano)
1 egg yolk, slightly beaten
1 tablespoon water
Caraway, sesame, and/or poppy seeds

- Preheat the oven to 350°F. Spray a baking sheet with vegetable oil spray. Set aside.

- In a large bowl beat the butter until smooth with an electric mixer or a wooden spoon. Gradually add the Parmesan cheese and sour cream. Mix well.

- Combine the flour and Italian seasoning. Gradually add to the cheese mixture, stirring with a wooden spoon until a smooth dough forms.

- Turn the dough out onto a lightly floured surface and divide in half. With a rolling pin, roll out half of the dough to a 12 x 6-inch rectangle and cut into 6 x $\frac{1}{2}$-inch strips. Twist each strip 2 to 3 times and place on the prepared baking sheet. Repeat with the rest of the dough.

- In a small bowl whisk the egg yolk and water until combined. Using a pastry brush, brush the strips lightly with the egg wash mixture, and sprinkle with seeds of choice.

- Bake for 10 to 12 minutes, or until lightly browned. Let cool on a wire rack.

Quick Bruschetta

The tomato mixture from this recipe is also excellent served alongside Sun-Dried Tomato Focaccia Bread with Olives, p. 67.

1	teaspoon plus 1 tablespoon olive oil
2	small Roma tomatoes, chopped
2	tablespoons fresh basil, thinly sliced
1	clove garlic, minced
1	teaspoon balsamic vinegar
	Salt and pepper to taste
6	small slices from a French baguette
	Crumbled goat cheese, if desired

Equipment
Small bowl
Pastry brush
Baking sheet

Servings
2

Preparation Time
10 minutes

Total Time
10 minutes

• In a small bowl mix 1 teaspoon of the olive oil with the chopped tomatoes, basil, garlic, and balsamic vinegar. Stir to blend thoroughly, and add salt and pepper to taste. Set aside.

• Using a pastry brush, brush the remaining 1 tablespoon olive oil across both sides of the bread slices. Put the bread on a baking sheet and put under the broiler for just a few minutes, until it starts to turn golden brown on top. Turn the bread over and broil other side just until golden brown. Remove from the oven.

• Arrange 3 slices of bread on each of two serving plates, and spoon some of the tomato mixture on top of each slice. Sprinkle with crumbled goat cheese, if desired.

Unplug the phone and turn off any beeping electronic gadgets during dinner.

Party Meatballs

A chafing dish set over hot water works great for keeping the meatballs warm during a party. Serve with toothpicks.

Equipment
Large bowl
Large skillet or saucepan

Servings
8 to 12

Preparation Time
30 minutes

Total Time
35 minutes

1   pound ground beef (10–15 percent fat)
1   cup dry breadcrumbs or crushed saltine crackers
1   egg
½   cup very finely minced yellow onion
1   teaspoon salt
1   teaspoon pepper
1   cup of your favorite barbecue sauce
⅓   cup pineapple juice (drain from a can of pineapple)

- In a large bowl combine the ground beef, breadcrumbs, egg, onion, salt, and pepper. With clean hands or a wooden spoon (hands work best), mix the beef mixture until it is completely combined.

- Shape the beef mixture into 1-inch balls, and place the balls on waxed paper. In a large skillet or saucepan with a lid place one layer of meatballs over medium-high heat. (You may need to cook in two or more batches, depending on the size of your skillet.)

- Cook the meatballs without stirring for about 2 to 3 minutes. Stir and turn over as many as possible. Let cook another 2 to 3 minutes. Continue cooking, stirring frequently, until well browned on all sides and completely cooked through.

- Remove the meatballs from the skillet to paper towels to drain. Cook the remaining meatballs the same way.

- Put all of the meatballs back in the skillet and add the barbecue sauce and pineapple juice. Cook, stirring frequently, for about 5 minutes, or until the sauce is hot and bubbling.

- Spoon the meatballs and sauce into a serving dish.

Mom's Tangy Cheese Ball

Crackers are the classic accompaniment to cheese balls, but try sliced green apples for a tangy contrast. Apples and cheese taste fabulous together.

½	pound sharp Cheddar cheese, grated
2	ounces blue cheese, crumbled
4	ounces cream cheese, softened
1	teaspoon Worcestershire sauce
1	teaspoon very finely minced onion
	Cayenne pepper to taste
¼	cup finely chopped pecans
¼	cup finely chopped parsley

- In a large bowl blend the Cheddar cheese, blue cheese, and cream cheese with an electric mixer or a wooden spoon until fairly uniform in texture and color. (A stand mixer with the paddle attachment works best, but a wooden spoon will do the job.) Add the Worcestershire sauce, minced onion, and cayenne pepper to taste. Chill the cheese mixture for at least one hour (and up to two days) in the refrigerator.

- With clean hands, form the cheese mixture into one or two balls. Mix the pecans and parsley and spread the mixture on waxed paper. Roll the cheese balls in the mixture until coated completely. Serve chilled or at room temperature with vegetable slices and crackers.

Set a complete table, including china, silverware, wine glasses, and napkins.

Note
Make sure all of the cheeses are at room temperature.

Equipment
Cheese grater
Electric mixer
Large bowl
Waxed paper

Servings
12

Serving Suggestions
- Crackers
- Vegetable slices
- Apple slices

Preparation Time
15 minutes

Total Time
1 hour 15 minutes

Jane's Mushroom-Almond Spread

This is kind of like a vegetarian paté. A departure from the ordinary appetizer, it is one of Jane's standards for her famous Valentine's Day party.

Equipment
Baking sheet
Large skillet
Food processor or blender

Servings
12

Serving Suggestions
• Crackers
• Vegetable slices

Preparation Time
20 minutes

Total Time
20 minutes

1	cup slivered almonds
¼	cup butter
1½	cups chopped onion
2	cloves garlic, minced
¾	pound button mushrooms, cleaned, trimmed, and sliced
¾	teaspoon salt
½	teaspoon thyme
¼	teaspoon pepper
2	tablespoons oil
	Mushroom slices (garnish)
	Kalamata olives (garnish)

- Preheat the oven to 350°F.

- Spread the almonds on a baking sheet; toast in the oven for 8 minutes or until lightly browned.

- Meanwhile, in a large skillet melt the butter over medium-high heat. Add the onion, garlic, mushrooms, salt, thyme, and pepper. Cook, stirring occasionally, until the onion is soft and the pan juices have evaporated.

- In a food processor or blender, blend the almonds to form a paste. With the blender still running, add the oil and mix until creamy. Add the mushroom mixture and blend just until smooth and fluffy.

- Spoon the mixture into a serving dish, and garnish with mushroom slices and Kalamata olives.

- Serve warm.

Queso Fundido

You just can't get much better than melted cheese, and this is so easy to make. Remember to toss the cheese with the flour, or your queso will end up as a big ball of cheese floating in beer.

1	pound (16 ounces) grated Monterey Jack cheese
¼	cup flour
1	cup beer
½	cup chopped fresh cilantro
4	teaspoons minced jalapeño peppers
¼	cup finely chopped red bell pepper
	Salt and pepper to taste
	Blue corn tortilla chips

- In a medium bowl combine the grated Monterey Jack cheese and flour, and toss to coat.

- In a large heavy saucepan bring the beer to a boil. Reduce the heat to low. Add a handful of cheese to the beer, stirring constantly until the cheese melts. Repeat with the remaining cheese. Stir until thick and creamy but do not boil. Stir in the cilantro, jalapeños, and red bell peppers, and season to taste with salt and pepper.

- Pour the cheese mixture into a flameproof baking dish or a disposable aluminum foil baking dish.

- Place the baking dish under the broiler until the top is golden-brown, about 2 minutes. Set the dish on a warming plate or over Sterno fuel on the serving table.

- Serve with chips.

Equipment
Cheese grater
Medium bowl
Large heavy saucepan
Flameproof baking dish or disposable aluminum foil baking dish

Serving Suggestions
Tortilla chips

Servings
12

Preparation Time
10 minutes

Total Time
12 minutes

Smoked Gouda and Prosciutto Wedges

Prosciutto (Italian ham) is available in specialty markets and the deli section of some supermarkets. If you can't find it, substitute good quality thinly sliced smoked deli ham.

Equipment
Medium skillet
Cheese grater
Large skillet
Baking sheet

Servings
4

Serving Suggestions
Fruity Pinot Grigio or
Riesling wine

Preparation Time
25 minutes

Total Time
30 minutes

2	tablespoons butter, divided
1	small yellow onion, thinly sliced
2	teaspoons brown sugar
½	teaspoon balsamic vinegar
1	cup (loosely packed) grated smoked Gouda cheese
3	ounces sliced prosciutto, chopped
	Salt and pepper to taste
2	10-inch-diameter flour tortillas

- Preheat the oven to 350°F.

- In a medium skillet melt 1 tablespoon butter over medium heat. Add the onion, brown sugar, and vinegar. Cook, stirring frequently, until the onion is golden brown and caramelized, about 15 minutes. Remove from the heat.

- Meanwhile, sprinkle the Gouda cheese and prosciutto on each tortilla, dividing equally, and season to taste with salt and pepper.

- When the onions are done, spread them on top of the cheese and prosciutto, and fold the tortillas over.

- In a large skillet melt the remaining 1 tablespoon butter over medium-high heat. Cook the tortillas one at a time until they start to turn golden-brown with browned spots, about 2 minutes per side. Add more butter to the skillet between tortillas, if necessary. Place on a baking sheet. Bake for about 5 minutes, until the cheese completely melts.

- Remove from the oven, and cut each tortilla into four triangles. Serve hot.

Speedy Guacamole

Buy avocados that are large, very green in color, and slightly soft to the touch. Too soft, and they are usually rotten; too firm, and they are hard as rocks. You can change the amount of salt and lime juice in the guacamole depending on the flavors that you like best.

2	ripe avocados
3	cloves garlic, peeled
3	tablespoons fresh lime juice
2	teaspoons salt

- Slice the avocados in half lengthwise and open them. Remove the pits. Using a tablespoon, scoop the meat of the avocados out of the skins (see p. 43), and put it in the food processor. Discard the skins.

- Add the garlic cloves to the processor on top of the avocado (if the garlic is underneath, it will just spin uncut at the bottom of the machine). Blend or chop until the mixture is smooth. (If you don't have a food processor, you can just use a medium bowl. Chop the garlic first and place the avocado and the garlic in the bowl. Mash with a fork until smooth.)

- Add the lime juice and salt, and blend or stir again until well mixed.

Tell your partner why you love them.

Equipment
Food processor or medium bowl and fork

Servings
6 to 8

Serving Suggestions
If you are a guacamole fan, you can serve it with anything (we even eat guacamole sandwiches). Guacamole always goes with any type of southwestern food, like Magical Southwestern Black Beans (p. 118), or just plain tortillas or tortilla chips.

Preparation Time
10 minutes

Total Time
10 minutes

Notes
Accént, also known as monosodium glutamate or MSG, is a flavor enhancer. This brand name product is widely available in the spice section of most supermarkets, but can be rather expensive. On the other hand, Asian food markets often carry 8-ounce or larger packages of MSG at very low prices.

Equipment
Several large ceramic, glass, or metal oven-safe mixing bowls
Large saucepan

Servings
24

Preparation Time
15

Total Time
1 hour 45 minutes

Grandma Ruby's Nuts and Bolts

Grandma Ruby called it Nuts and Bolts rather than the more common name of "Chex Mix" because of how the pretzels and Cheerios look together!

1	16-ounce box Wheat Chex cereal
1	16-ounce box Bran Chex cereal
1	12-ounce box Corn Chex cereal
1	12-ounce box Cheerios cereal
1	12-ounce bag pretzel sticks
1	8-ounce bag Goldfish crackers
16	ounces dry-roasted salted peanuts
1	pound (4 sticks) butter, melted
1	tablespoon garlic powder
1	tablespoon curry powder
3	tablespoons chili powder
1	tablespoon MSG or Accént, optional
½	cup Worcestershire sauce

- Preheat the oven to 150°F (or "warm" setting).

- Evenly mix cereals, pretzels, Goldfish crackers, and peanuts together in several large ceramic, glass, or metal oven-safe bowls. (If you have a bowl large enough to fit everything at once, you can use it instead, as long as it will fit in your oven.)

- In a large saucepan melt the butter over medium heat. Stir in the garlic powder, curry powder, chili powder, MSG, and Worcestershire sauce. Increase the heat to high and bring to a boil. Reduce the heat to low and simmer for 3 minutes longer. Pour the mixture evenly over the cereal, stirring from the bottom to mix and coat thoroughly.

- Bake in the warm oven for 90 minutes, stirring thoroughly from the bottom every 15 minutes. Let cool.

- Store the Nuts and Bolts in plastic zipper-top bags or food storage containers.

Pepper-Ranch Cheese Ball

This was one of Katy's mom's standard party items, and a crowd favorite. The longer it sits in the refrigerator before serving, the better it tastes. You can substitute Lawry's Seasoned Pepper for the spice mixture used to coat the cheese balls.

16	ounces cream cheese
1	package Hidden Valley Ranch dressing mix
2	tablespoons ground black pepper
1	teaspoon sugar
1	teaspoon paprika
2	teaspoons salt

- In a medium bowl mix together the cream cheese and ranch dressing mix with a wooden spoon. With clean hands, roll the mixture into a ball.

- In a bowl slightly bigger than the cheese ball mix together the pepper, sugar, paprika, and salt. Roll the cheese ball in the pepper mixture to coat thoroughly. You can just shake and bounce it around gently in the bowl, and it should turn and coat itself fairly well.

- Wrap the cheese ball in plastic wrap, making sure it is airtight, and refrigerate for at least 24 hours, and up to 3 days.

- Serve chilled.

Invite your favorite couple and cook for four.

Equipment
Medium bowl
Small bowl

Serving Suggestions
- Crackers
- Vegetable slices

Servings
16

Preparation Time
15 minutes

Total Time
15 minutes (plus chill time in the refrigerator of at least one day)

Tex-Mex Won Tons

Deeelicious! An unusual blend of flavors to find in a won ton. They are on the mild side heat-wise, but you can spice them up by adding cayenne pepper or a chopped jalapeño pepper to the filling. Won ton wrappers can be found at Asian food markets or in the refrigerated or produce section of most supermarkets.

Equipment
Large skillet
Deep fryer or large deep
skillet

Servings
16

Preparation Time
30 minutes

Total Time
1 hour

½	pound ground beef
¼	cup chopped onion
2	tablespoons chopped green pepper
7½	ounces refried beans (half of a 15-ounce can)
¼	cup shredded Cheddar cheese
1	tablespoon ketchup
1½	teaspoons chili powder
¼	teaspoon ground cumin
48	won ton wrappers
	Vegetable oil for frying
	Salsa
	Sour cream

- In a large skillet over medium-high heat cook the ground beef, onion, and green pepper until the meat is browned and the vegetables are tender. Drain off the fat. Stir the beans, cheese, ketchup, chili powder, and cumin into the meat mixture. Mix well.

- Place a won ton wrapper on a clean counter with one point toward you. Spoon a generous teaspoon of filling onto the center of the wrapper. Fold the nearest point toward the center of the filling. Fold the side corners over, forming an envelope shape. Roll up toward the remaining corner, moisten the point, and press to seal. Repeat with the remaining won ton wrappers and filling.

- Pour the vegetable oil into a large deep skillet to a depth of at least 1 inch, or use a deep fryer. Heat to 375°F. Fry the won-tons a few at a time (about 1 minute per side) until golden brown. Drain on paper towels. Serve immediately with salsa and sour cream.

Breads

Garlic Bread

An even quicker and easier variation: Omit the garlic. Spread the bread with plain butter, then sprinkle with garlic salt. Broil as directed.

4	slices hearty wheat, white, or French bread
4	teaspoons butter, softened
1	clove garlic, finely minced
	Salt and pepper to taste

- Arrange the bread slices on a baking sheet.

- In a small bowl combine the butter and minced garlic, stirring to blend thoroughly. Evenly spread one side of each bread slice with the garlic butter. Sprinkle with salt and pepper to taste.

- Place the bread slices under the broiler and broil for 2 to 3 minutes, watching very carefully to avoid burning them. Remove from the broiler and serve.

Keep a bottle of your favorite champagne chilled in the refrigerator for whenever a romantic mood strikes you.

Equipment
Small bowl
Baking sheet

Serving Suggestions
What *doesn't* garlic bread go with?! We love it with any kind of Italian food, or with grilled vegetables, chicken, fish, or soup.

Servings
2

Preparation Time
5 minutes

Total Time
5 minutes

Braided Scarborough Fair Bread

This bread is absolutely heavenly served warm from the oven with butter.

Equipment
Large bowl
Electric mixer
Medium saucepan
2 small bowls
Baking sheet

Servings
2 loaves

Preparation Time
35 minutes

Total Time
3 hours

6½ to 7½ cups all-purpose flour

2   packages dry yeast

3   tablespoons sugar

1   tablespoon salt

¼   cup dried parsley flakes

1   teaspoon dried rosemary, crumbled

1   teaspoon dried thyme

⅓   cup dried onion flakes

1   cup plus 1 tablespoon milk

1   cup water

¼   cup (½ stick) butter

2   eggs

⅓   cup poppy and/or sesame seeds

• In a large bowl combine 2 cups of the flour with the yeast, sugar, salt, parsley, rosemary and thyme.

• In a medium saucepan combine the onion flakes, 1 cup milk, water, and butter over medium-low heat. Heat until warm, but do not allow it to boil or simmer. The butter does not need to melt completely.

• Add the warm liquid to the flour mixture. Beat for 2 minutes at medium speed with an electric mixer.

• In a small bowl lightly beat the eggs. Measure out 2 tablespoons of the beaten eggs into another small bowl, and set it aside. Pour the remaining eggs into the dough, and beat well.

• Gradually add the remaining flour in ½ cup increments, mixing until a thick dough forms. Knead the dough until smooth and elastic. Let the dough rise in an oiled bowl, covered with a kitchen towel, in a warm place for approximately 1 hour, or until it has about doubled in size.

Bring home a big bouquet of freshly picked wildflowers as a surprise for your partner.

- Shape the bread: Form 2 braids by dividing the dough into 6 equal pieces. Roll each piece out into a strand about 12 to 14 inches long, and braid three strands together, carefully tucking in the ends. Repeat with the three remaining pieces. Let the loaves rise again on a greased baking sheet for about an hour, covered.

- Preheat the oven to 375°F.

- Mix 1 tablespoon milk into the reserved 2 tablespoons of eggs. Brush the mixture on top of the bread and sprinkle with the seeds.

- Bake the loaves for 20 to 30 minutes or until golden.

Get your pictures taken together in a photo booth. Act silly. Kiss during at least one picture. Frame the photos and put them on your dinner table.

Debra's Simple Beer Bread

This recipe makes a rather dense bread that goes well with soups. And it's just about the easiest "from-scratch" bread you can make.

3	cups all-purpose flour
3¾	teaspoons baking powder
¼	teaspoon salt
2	tablespoons sugar
1	12-ounce can beer (not light beer), room temperature
2	tablespoons butter, melted

Equipment
Large bowl
Loaf pan

Servings
4 to 6

Preparation Time
15 minutes

Total Time
1 hour 15 minutes

- Preheat the oven to 375°F. Generously grease a metal loaf pan.

- In a large bowl mix the flour, baking powder, salt, and sugar with the beer until just blended.

- Spoon the dough into the prepared loaf pan, smoothing the top into a nice rounded form. Bake for 45 to 60 minutes, until the top is browned.

- Remove from the oven. Brush the top with melted butter. Remove from the pan and cover with a towel while cooling.

Use real, matching plates, bowls, and glasses.

Sun-Dried Tomato Focaccia Bread with Olives

Focaccia bread is delicious served hot as a snack or an appetizer, or as part of an Italian meal. Using oil from the sun-dried tomatoes lends a stronger tomato flavor and a beautiful golden-orange color to the bread.

4   cups flour

2   packages yeast

1   tablespoon Italian seasoning (or use thyme, basil, or oregano)

¼   cup chopped sun-dried tomatoes in oil, drained

½   cup pitted Kalamata olives, chopped

2   tablespoons olive oil (or oil from the tomatoes)

1½ to 2 cups warm (not hot) water

Extra olive oil for drizzling

Herbs of choice (such as basil, rosemary, oregano, or thyme)

Sea salt and coarsely ground pepper to taste

Equipment
9 x 13-inch pan or glass baking dish
Large mixing bowl

Servings
8

Preparation Time
25 minutes

Total Time
1 hour 40 minutes

• Lightly grease a 9 x 13-inch pan or glass baking dish. In a large mixing bowl stir together the flour, yeast, Italian seasoning, sun-dried tomatoes, olives, and oil. Add 1½ cups warm water. Stir well. Add more water, if necessary, until the dough forms a ball.

• Turn the dough out onto a floured surface. Knead until smooth and elastic, about 10 minutes, adding as little flour as possible to keep it from sticking. Place the dough in an oiled bowl to rise, about 30 to 45 minutes.

• Preheat the oven to 450°F. Flatten the dough in the prepared pan all the way to the edges; cover with a towel. Let it rise in a warm place for about 20 minutes. Drizzle with olive oil and sprinkle with herbs, salt, and pepper.

• Bake 12 to 15 minutes, or until lightly browned and puffy. Serve warm.

Katy's Grilled Pizza Crusts

Equipment
Barbecue grill
Small bowl
Large mixing bowl or
  stand mixer
Rolling pin

Serving Suggestions
- These are great with just a sprinkling of sea salt, cracked black pepper, and Gruyere cheese.
- Serve with a green salad.

Servings
4

Preparation Time
35 minutes

Total Time
2 hours 15 minutes

1	tablespoon dry yeast (quick-rising is OK)
	Pinch brown sugar
1¼	cups warm water
2	tablespoons olive or sun-dried tomato oil
¼	teaspoon pepper
1½	teaspoons garlic salt
1	teaspoon dried oregano
1	teaspoon dried basil
1	teaspoon fennel seeds, crushed (optional)
¼	cup oil-packed sun-dried tomatoes, drained and chopped
3	or more cups white or whole wheat flour

- In a small bowl dissolve the yeast and sugar in the warm water. When the yeast bubbles to the surface (5 to 10 minutes), mix in the olive oil, pepper, garlic salt, oregano, basil, fennel seeds, and sun-dried tomatoes.

- Pour the mixture into a large mixing bowl or the bowl of a stand mixer. Gradually mix in the flour by the half-cup. Add more flour, if necessary, to make a stiff but smooth dough.

- Knead the dough well until it becomes smooth and elastic. Place the dough in an oiled bowl and let it rise in a warm place, about 1½ hours (45 minutes for quick-rising yeast).

- Remove the dough from the bowl. Punch it down and knead well again, about 3 to 4 minutes. Divide the dough into four pieces, and roll out with a rolling pin into 8-inch crusts. Let the dough relax for a few minutes; it will spring back. Roll out again to about 8-inch size.

- Preheat the grill to medium. Brush both sides of the dough rounds with olive oil. Carefully set the crusts onto the hot grill; they will immediately firm up and begin to bubble. Cook for about 4 minutes, until the dough is lightly browned and has grill marks on the

Get the old-fashioned stove-top popcorn for an after dinner snack.

bottom. Flip the crusts over and add your choice of tomato sauce, cheese, and toppings. Cover the grill and cook for an additional 3 to 4 minutes, or until the cheese melts.

- *Note:* To freeze for later use, cook the crusts on both sides for about 4 minutes. Let cool, wrap tightly in plastic, and freeze. Let the frozen crusts thaw for two hours at room temperature before using. When ready, add toppings of choice and grill or broil until the cheese melts.

Eat chocolate off your partner's ... plate.

Finish off an entire bottle of wine between the two of you.

Jane's Easy Biscuits

Equipment
Medium bowl
Small bowl
Baking sheet

Servings
8

Serving Suggestions
Serve hot with butter and jam or honey.

Preparation Time
10 minutes

Total Time
25 minutes

2	cups white flour
1	tablespoon sugar
$\frac{1}{2}$	teaspoon salt
3	teaspoons baking powder
$\frac{1}{2}$	cup shortening
1	egg
$\frac{3}{4}$	cup milk

- Preheat the oven to 450°F. Lightly grease a baking sheet.

- In a medium bowl combine the flour, sugar, salt, and baking powder. Add the shortening. Use a fork or a pastry blender to mix the shortening in, just until the mixture resembles small pebbles.

- In a small bowl whisk the egg until light yellow in color, and stir in the milk. Gradually pour this mixture into the bowl with the flour mixture, and stir until it is combined.

- Drop the biscuit dough by tablespoonfuls onto the prepared baking sheet. Bake for 10 to 14 minutes, or until golden. Serve hot with butter and jam.

Fresh flowers will make any dining table beautiful and romantic.

Main Courses

Mediterranean Shrimp Fettuccine

- 4 ounces fettuccine
- 2 tablespoons butter
- 2 cloves garlic, minced
- ¼ cup dry white wine
- ½ pound medium shrimp, peeled and deveined
- 1 small Roma tomato, diced
- ½ teaspoon dried oregano leaves
- 2 teaspoons lemon juice
- 2 ounces feta cheese, crumbled coarsely (about ¼ cup)
  Parmesan cheese, shredded

- In a large pot of boiling salted water cook the fettuccine until tender but still firm to bite. Drain.

- Meanwhile, in a large skillet heat the butter, garlic, and wine over medium heat until the butter is melted. Add the peeled and deveined shrimp, tomato, and oregano. Increase the heat to medium-high and cook for 3 to 4 minutes, or until the shrimp are opaque and cooked through. (If you cook them too long they will turn tough.)

- Remove the skillet from the heat and stir in the lemon juice and feta cheese. Spoon over the pasta and sprinkle with Parmesan cheese.

Equipment
Large pot
Large skillet

Serving Suggestions
- Crusty bread
- Spinach salad
- Chilled white wine or sparkling apple juice

Servings
2

Preparation Time
10 minutes

Total Time
15 minutes

Mother-in-Law's Shrimp Curry

This recipe works fast, sort of like stir-fry, so have everything ready to cook before heating the stove. Garam masala is available at Indian markets or in the Asian or spice section of many supermarkets.

3	tablespoons vegetable oil
1	tablespoon cumin seeds
2	tablespoons fresh ginger, chopped
1	tablespoon dried red chilies or red pepper flakes (optional)
1	medium onion, chopped
4	large tomatoes, chopped
½	pound shrimp, any size, peeled and deveined
2	teaspoons turmeric
1	teaspoon ground cumin
1	teaspoon ground coriander
1	teaspoon garam masala powder
2	to 3 teaspoons salt
¼	cup cilantro, chopped (garnish)

- In a heavy saucepan heat the oil over medium-high heat. Add the cumin seeds, ginger, and dried red chilies (if you are using them). Stand back, as the pan gets lively and pungent. Let it cook for about a minute, but don't let it overheat, or it will burn.

- Add the chopped onions and tomatoes. Let them cook until softened, stirring often, for at least 5 minutes.

- Add the peeled and deveined shrimp. They will begin to turn opaque almost immediately. Stir in the turmeric, ground cumin, coriander, garam masala, and salt, and mix well. Reduce the heat to low.

- Let the whole pot cook for about 20 minutes, stirring occasionally. The dish will create its own broth.

- Garnish with the chopped cilantro and serve over hot steamed rice.

Note
A curry, by definition, is a dish with sauce, not the yellow powder you get in the spice section of the supermarket.

Variations
This dish is almost limitless in its adaptability. You can add as little or as much spice as you like, with as few or as many shrimp. The idea remains the same: to meld the flavors of the seafood into the juiciness of the vegetables, much like an étouffée.

Equipment
Heavy saucepan

Servings
2

Serving Suggestions
- Hot steamed rice
- Serve this dish with a hearty red wine, like Merlot or Chianti. Open the bottle as you start cooking to allow the wine to "breathe."

Preparation Time
10 minutes

Total Time
30 minutes

Dad's No-Mess Salmon in a Packet

Salmon is a wonderfully hearty fish, but be careful of the bones when eating—many are tiny. Buy the brightest and freshest salmon you can find.

2	cloves garlic
¾	pound fresh salmon fillet
½	cup white wine or Sherry cooking wine
2	tablespoons butter
	Salt and pepper to taste
	Rosemary or other herbs of your choice

Equipment
Aluminum foil or dispos-
able foil baking dish
Baking sheet or dish

Serving Suggestions
• Spicy Potato Gratin
(p. 169)
• Fast Fresh Fruit Salad
(p. 141)
• Try this trick: Top off
half a glass of your
favorite fruit juice with
plain sparkling water,
like Perrier. It makes a
nice bubbly, non-
alcoholic addition to
your meal. Apple,
grape, or even orange
juice work well for
this.

Servings
2

Preparation Time
10 minutes

Total Time
30 minutes

• Preheat the oven to 350°F. With the heel of your hand, gently smash the garlic cloves under the flat of a large knife blade. Remove the peel.

• Briefly rinse the salmon under cold running water and pat dry with paper towels. Lay a large sheet of foil (large enough to close over the fish) on a baking sheet. Alternately, you can use a disposable tinfoil baking dish. Place the salmon in the center of the foil. Bring up the edges so that the liquid does not run out, and pour the white wine or cooking Sherry over the fish. Place the butter and garlic on top of the salmon and sprinkle with salt, pepper, and rosemary or other herbs of your choice.

• Close up the foil at the top, folding over to seal. Bring up both sides, folding over several times to seal securely. Make sure it is completely sealed, otherwise the wine will evaporate and the fish will dry out. If using a disposable dish, cover securely with a sheet of foil and crimp the edges to seal.

• Place the fish package on the baking sheet in the preheated oven, and bake for 20 to 22 minutes. (If it cooks too long, the fish will become tough.) Remove from the oven and open the foil carefully. Check the salmon by cutting open at the thickest part and making sure it is opaque all the way through.

• Cut the fish into two pieces and serve.

Pan-Grilled Halibut

If you are missing any of the spices for this recipe, you may leave them out and still achieve a good flavor. We've found that this is a rather tasty blend.

Equipment
Small bowl
Medium saucepan with lid

Serving Suggestions
- Steamed rice or garlic bread
- Sautéed Green Beans (p. 166)
- Chilled white wine such as Chardonnay or Chablis

Servings
2

Preparation Time
15 minutes

Total Time
15 minutes

¼	teaspoon allspice
1	teaspoon dried basil
½	teaspoon dried thyme
½	teaspoon dried oregano
½	teaspoon garlic salt
½	teaspoon ground black pepper
¼	teaspoon sage
1	tablespoon dried onion flakes
2	6-ounce halibut steaks, about 1-inch thick
4	tablespoons olive oil

- In a small bowl combine the allspice, basil, thyme, oregano, garlic salt, pepper, sage, and onion flakes.

- Briefly rinse the halibut under cold running water and pat dry with paper towels.

- In a medium saucepan (big enough to hold both fish steaks) heat two tablespoons olive oil over medium-high heat. When hot, place the fish in the pan. Drizzle the remaining 2 tablespoons oil on top of the fish, and sprinkle with the spice mixture.

- Cook the fish, uncovered, for about 2 minutes on each side. Cover the pan and cook for an additional 2 minutes on each side with the pan covered, or until the fish is cooked through. Check the fish by cutting open at the thickest part and making sure it is opaque all the way through.

- Remove the fish from the pan and serve immediately.

Bob's Poached Fish on the Grill

Katy got this recipe from her boss. He prefers to use prepackaged frozen vegetables for convenience's sake, but we find that fresh ones taste much better.

2	6-ounce whitefish fillets, such as orange roughy
½	cup chopped onion
½	bell pepper, any color, chopped
2	cloves garlic, minced
4	medium-sized button mushrooms, sliced (about ½ cup)
	Salt and pepper to taste
⅔	cup white wine or chicken broth

- Preheat the barbecue grill to medium-high. For this recipe, you can use either disposable tinfoil baking dishes or aluminum foil.

- If using aluminum foil, tear off a sheet approximately 18 inches long. Fold in half. Fold up all four sides about 1½ inches, securing the corners, to make a shallow rectangular tray to fit one fish fillet. Repeat with a second sheet of foil.

- Spray the bottoms of the trays with nonstick cooking spray.

- Briefly rinse the fish fillets under cold running water and pat dry with paper towels. Place a fillet in each tray.

- Sprinkle fillets with the onion, bell pepper, garlic, and mushrooms. Sprinkle with salt and pepper to taste and pour ⅓ cup wine or chicken broth over each.

- Place the trays on the grill and let cook for approximately 10 minutes. Check the fish by cutting open at the thickest part and making sure it is opaque all the way through.

- Remove the fish and vegetables from the trays and place on plates. Drizzle with pan juices. Serve hot.

Equipment
Aluminum foil or disposable tinfoil baking dishes
Barbecue grill

Serving Suggestions
- Garlic Bread (p. 63)
- Grilled Vegetables (p. 170)
- White wine

Preparation Time
5 minutes

Total Time
15 minutes

Crispy-Bottomed Salmon with Balsamic Sauce

Salmon is a good fish to cook because, as fish goes, it has a relatively high fat content, making it very flavorful and easy to work with. The oil naturally found in fish is the "good" kind, called omega-3 fatty acids. When frying foods in oil, keep a small bowl of white vinegar sitting nearby to cut down on the smell.

1	small or medium orange
$\frac{1}{2}$	cup orange juice
$\frac{1}{4}$	cup balsamic vinegar
2	tablespoons olive oil
1	tablespoon finely chopped onion
1	teaspoon chopped parsley
$\frac{1}{4}$	teaspoon salt
$\frac{1}{4}$	teaspoon pepper
2	6-ounce skinless fillets of salmon, 1 to $1\frac{1}{2}$ inches thick
	Salt and pepper to taste

• Preheat the oven to 450°F.

• With the fine holes of a cheese grater or with a citrus-zesting tool, grate about 1 tablespoon of the peel from the orange, being careful not to grate any of the white pith. Cut the orange into slices and set aside.

• In a jar with a tight-fitting lid combine the orange zest, orange juice, vinegar, 1 tablespoon of the olive oil, onion, parsley, salt, and pepper. Put lid on and shake vigorously until well blended. Set aside.

• Briefly rinse the salmon under cold running water and pat dry with paper towels. Season with salt and pepper to taste.

• In a large oven-proof skillet heat the remaining 1 tablespoon of olive oil over high heat. Place the salmon in the pan, skin side down (the salmon is skinless but it should be obvious which side had the skin). Cook for

2 minutes without lifting or stirring the fish. You may wish to use a splatter screen, if you have one, because the oil may splatter.

- Place the pan with the salmon in the oven and roast for approximately 10 to 12 minutes. Check for doneness by slicing open the thickest part of the fillet. It is cooked through when opaque at the center. The bottom of the salmon should be nice and crispy.

- Remove the skillet from the oven, and put the fish on a serving plate, covered loosely with aluminum foil to keep warm.

- Discard the oil from the skillet, and put the skillet back on the stove over high heat. Pour the orange-balsamic sauce into the hot pan. Cook for about 30 seconds or until it is bubbling. Spoon the sauce over the salmon, garnish with orange slices, and serve.

Bring home your partner's favorite ice cream. Serve it with chocolate mints.

Tell each other the story of how you first met.

Mermaid's Delight Rice Bowls

Frozen microwaveable rice bowls are very popular these days, but it's quite easy to make your own at home. The technique is the same: layer freshly steamed rice with meat and/or vegetables, topping with any number of spices, sauces, or condiments.

Equipment
Medium saucepan with lid
Large skillet

Servings
2

Preparation Time
10 minutes

Total Time
30 minutes

1	cup rice
2	cups water
1	teaspoon chicken or vegetable bouillon (or 1 cube)
2	teaspoons olive oil
1	clove garlic, minced
½	pound medium shrimp, peeled and deveined
1	6-ounce can crabmeat, drained
⅔	cup canned corn, drained
1	Roma tomato, chopped
2	tablespoons sun-dried tomatoes in oil, drained and chopped
½	cup grated Monterey Jack cheese
3	tablespoons fresh basil leaves, sliced

- In a medium saucepan combine the rice, water, and bouillon over high heat. Bring to a boil. Reduce the heat to medium-low, cover the pan, and cook without stirring for about 20 minutes, or until the rice is tender and the liquid is absorbed.

- Meanwhile, in a large skillet heat the olive oil over medium-high heat. Add the garlic, shrimp, and crabmeat. Sauté until the shrimp are opaque and cooked through, about 4 minutes. Add salt and pepper to taste.

- In two serving bowls, layer the ingredients in this order: hot rice, seafood mixture, corn, Roma tomatoes, sun-dried tomatoes, and Monterey Jack cheese. Season to taste with salt and pepper, and sprinkle with basil to garnish.

Roasted Fish with Olives

3	tablespoons olive oil
2	fish steaks (such as tuna, halibut, or swordfish), about 1 inch thick and ½ pound each
2	cloves garlic, minced
	Salt and pepper to taste
¼	cup white wine vinegar
¼	cup sliced green or Kalamata olives
1	tablespoon chopped fresh parsley

- Preheat the oven to 400°F. Pour 1 tablespoon olive oil into an 8-inch square glass baking dish to coat the bottom thoroughly.

- Briefly rinse the fish under cold running water and pat dry with paper towels.

- Place the fish in the prepared baking dish, and sprinkle with minced garlic, salt, and pepper. Drizzle with vinegar and the remaining 2 tablespoons oil, and arrange the olives on top of the fish.

- Bake, uncovered, for 15 minutes. Check for doneness by cutting the fish open at the thickest part and making sure it is opaque all the way through.

- Transfer to a serving platter. Pour the pan juices over the fish and sprinkle with parsley. Serve immediately.

Do the dishes when it's not your turn.

Equipment
8-inch square glass baking dish

Servings
2

Serving Suggestions
- Plain pasta with garlic and olive oil, basil, and Parmesan cheese
- A nice Greek wine

Preparation Time
5 minutes

Total Time
20 minutes

Teriyaki Scampi

"Scampi" is simply a term referring to shrimp sautéed in butter. This can also be used as an appetizer.

2	tablespoons soy sauce
2	teaspoons Sherry cooking wine
1	teaspoon brown sugar
½	teaspoon ground ginger
¼	teaspoon garlic powder
½	pound large shrimp, peeled and deveined
2	teaspoons butter
⅓	cup thinly sliced green onions
1	small clove garlic, minced
1	Roma tomato, chopped

- In a medium bowl mix the soy sauce, Sherry, brown sugar, ginger, and garlic powder. Add the peeled and deveined shrimp and marinate for 10 minutes.

- Reserving 2 tablespoons of the marinade, drain the shrimp thoroughly.

- In a medium skillet heat the butter on medium heat until it melts. Add the green onions and garlic and stir for 1 minute. Add the tomatoes and cook, stirring, for 3 minutes. Add the shrimp and reserved marinade. Cook, stirring frequently, for another 4 minutes or until the shrimp turn opaque.

- Remove from the heat and transfer to a serving bowl.

Equipment
Medium bowl
Medium skillet

Serving Suggestions
- Serve over hot cooked rice or pasta.
- Serve with green or jasmine tea. Use tea bowls (tea cups without handles) if you have them. They can be purchased in many home stores and Asian markets. Tea bowls are especially comforting on a cold night because they are meant to be used as hand warmers.

Servings
2

Preparation Time
15 minutes

Total Time
25 minutes

Speedy Sausage and Sauerkraut

Sauerkraut with sausage is a classic German dish. We've cheated a little by using a fully cooked kielbasa, but you can substitute your favorite kind of sausage. This recipe makes enough for leftovers, which are great on toasted rye bread for sandwiches.

1	24-ounce jar sauerkraut
16	ounces fully cooked kielbasa sausage
1	large onion, thinly sliced
1	cup chicken broth
3	tablespoons Dijon or German mustard
½	teaspoon allspice
½	teaspoon nutmeg

- Preheat the oven to 350°F.

- Put the sauerkraut in a colander or strainer, and rinse under cool running water to wash away as much of the brine as possible. Let it drain while you cook the sausage.

- Slice the kielbasa sausage into ¼-inch to ½-inch pieces. In a large ovenproof (or regular) skillet cook the sausage over medium-high heat, stirring frequently, until it begins to turn brown, about 5 to 7 minutes. Remove the sausage with a slotted spoon and drain on paper towels. Pour off the grease into an empty metal can and discard, leaving 1 tablespoon in the skillet.

- Add the sliced onion to the skillet and sauté until soft, about 5 minutes. Add the sauerkraut, chicken broth, mustard, allspice, and nutmeg. Turn the heat to high and bring to a boil. Return the sausage to the pan and let everything boil for 2 to 3 minutes.

- Remove the skillet from the heat. If your skillet is ovenproof, cover it with a lid or aluminum foil and place it in the oven. If not, transfer the sausage and sauerkraut to a 9 x 13-inch baking dish, cover it with a lid or aluminum foil, and place it in the oven. Bake for 20 minutes.

- Remove the pan from the oven and let stand for about 5 minutes before serving.

Equipment
Strainer or colander
Large ovenproof skillet or large skillet and 9 x 13-inch baking dish

Servings
4 to 6

Serving Suggestions
- Toasted bread or rolls
- Imported German beer
- The leftovers make great Reuben sandwiches. Toast slices of rye bread, spread with thousand island dressing, and pile on the sausage and sauerkraut. Yum!
- For a romantic treat, serve this with sparkling apple juice (like Martinelli's) for an authentic taste of Bavaria.

Preparation Time
25 minutes

Total Time
45 minutes

Smoky Black Beans and Rice with Sausage

Equipment
2 medium saucepans

Servings
2

Preparation Time
15 minutes

Total Time
25 minutes

1	cup long-grain white rice
2	cups water
4	ounces smoked sausage, sliced
½	cup onion, chopped finely
2	cloves garlic, minced
1	tablespoon Sherry cooking wine
½	teaspoon liquid smoke
1	15-ounce can black beans
½	teaspoon Tony C.'s Creole seasoning (or other seasoned salt)
½	teaspoon honey
2	teaspoons seasoned rice vinegar
2	tablespoons sour cream
	Green onions or chives, chopped, as garnish

- In a medium saucepan place the rice and water, and bring to a boil over high heat. Reduce the heat to medium-low, cover the pot, and let the rice simmer until it is cooked through and all the water is absorbed, about 15 to 20 minutes. Don't stir the rice or lift the lid while it's cooking.

- Meanwhile, in a medium nonstick saucepan, cook the sausage with the onions and garlic over medium heat, covered, stirring occasionally, until the sausage begins to brown. Add the Sherry and liquid smoke, stir, and cover. Cook about 2 minutes, until the liquid has slightly reduced. Add the black beans with their juices, Tony C.'s seasoning, honey, and vinegar. Simmer, stirring occasionally, for 10 to 15 minutes.

- Serve the beans and sausage over the hot fresh rice. Garnish each bowl with 1 tablespoon sour cream and a sprinkle of green onions or chives on top.

Crumbly Hamburger Sandwiches

When Katy was a kid, this was one of her favorite cold-weather quick suppers. It is easy to make, and it's true comfort food, though not especially healthy.

½ pound lean ground beef (sirloin or 10 percent fat or less)

¼ cup mayonnaise

2 tablespoons yellow mustard

   Salt and pepper to taste

2 thick hearty hamburger buns (onion buns are nice)

- In a skillet cook the ground beef over medium-high heat until browned and cooked through. Crumble it up into small pieces with the back of a wooden spoon while it cooks.

- When the beef is nicely browned, pour off the grease into an empty metal can by holding the beef back with a slotted spoon or strainer. Return the skillet to the stove. Stir in the mayonnaise and mustard, and cook just until heated through. Season to taste with salt and pepper.

- Meanwhile, toast the hamburger buns in a toaster oven or under the oven broiler until golden-brown and crisp.

- Spoon the meat mixture onto buns and serve hot.

Equipment
Skillet

Servings
2

Serving Suggestions
- If you are feeling creative, you could add some chopped onion and green pepper to the beef while it is cooking.
- Serve with potato chips and Coke for that true "I'm a kid again" feeling.

Preparation Time
10 minutes

Total Time
10 minutes

Shyamal's Breakfast Burritos

This recipe takes some logistical effort, but it gets faster the more often you make it, which you will definitely want to do. And these burritos are not just for breakfast! Serve them with waffles and fruit for an extra-special dinner.

Equipment
Small bowl
Large skillet

Servings
2 hungry people

Serving Suggestions
• Hot, dark coffee
• Waffles or Mom's Cinnamon Rolls (p. 196)
• Fast Fresh Fruit Salad (p. 141)

Preparation Time
25 minutes

Total Time
25 minutes

2 eggs
3 tablespoons milk
½ teaspoon oregano
½ teaspoon basil
½ teaspoon chili powder
½ cup grated Cheddar or Monterey Jack cheese
Salt and pepper to taste
4 ounces sausage, crumbled (we recommend chorizo or other spicy sausage)
1 clove garlic, minced
½ cup onion, minced
1 small Roma tomato, diced
2 9-inch diameter flour tortillas
Salsa (optional)

• In a small bowl beat the eggs with a whisk until frothy. Add the milk, oregano, basil, chili powder, 2 tablespoons of the cheese, and salt and pepper to taste. Mix well and set aside.

• In a large skillet cook the sausage over medium-high heat, stirring frequently, for about 10 minutes or until completely cooked. Remove the sausage with a slotted spoon and drain on paper towels. Pour off the grease into an empty metal can and discard, leaving 1 teaspoon in the skillet.

• Add the minced garlic to the skillet and cook on medium heat for about 30 seconds, stirring. Add the onions and cook until softened, about 2 minutes longer. Add the diced tomato and cook, stirring, an additional 2 minutes.

- Add the egg mixture to the skillet, and stir frequently until the eggs are scrambled. (Do not overcook, or the eggs will turn out dry.) Remove from the heat.

- Spoon half of the sausage and then half of the eggs down the center of each tortilla. Sprinkle with the remaining cheese and salt and pepper to taste. Roll up and serve with salsa.

Our Favorite Romantic Dinner Movies

An Affair to Remember	Love Story
Somewhere in Time	When Harry Met Sally
A Midsummer Night's Dream	Like Water for Chocolate
Four Weddings and a Funeral	Say Anything
Roman Holiday	The Princess Bride
Casablanca	An Officer and a Gentleman
Gone with the Wind	Ghost
Chasing Amy	

☆Orange Chicken Pasta

Equipment
Large saucepan
Cheese grater or citrus
  zesting tool
Medium bowl
Small bowl
Skillet

Servings
2

Preparation Time
25 minutes

Total Time
30 minutes

4	ounces angel hair pasta
3	teaspoons butter
2	boneless skinless chicken breasts
1	small or medium orange
½	cup orange juice
1	teaspoon cornstarch
2	tablespoons cider vinegar
1	teaspoon honey
½	teaspoon chicken bouillon granules
	Pepper to taste
1	cup sliced fresh mushrooms
½	cup sliced yellow onion
1	tablespoon butter
2	tablespoons sliced green onions or chives

• In a large pot of boiling salted water cook the pasta until tender but still firm to bite. Angel hair cooks fast, so taste it every minute or so until it is done. Drain. In a medium bowl toss the pasta and 1 teaspoon butter until the butter melts and the pasta is coated. Keep the pasta warm in an oven set on low.

• Briefly rinse the chicken under cold running water and pat dry with paper towels. Slice the chicken into ⅛-inch thick slices. This is easier to do when the chicken is still partially frozen.

• With the fine holes of a cheese grater or with a citrus-zesting tool grate about 1 tablespoon of the peel from the orange, being careful not to grate any of the white pith. Cut the orange into slices and set aside.

• In a small bowl combine 1 teaspoon of the orange juice with the cornstarch. Stir until completely blended and smooth. Gradually add the remaining orange juice. Stir in the orange peel, vinegar, honey, bouillon, and pepper to taste. Set aside.

Eat dinner in your fancy underwear.

- In a skillet cook the mushrooms and onion in the remaining 2 teaspoons of butter over medium-high heat, until softened and the mushrooms start to brown, about 5 minutes, stirring occasionally. Remove the mushroom-onion mixture from the skillet with a slotted spoon and add it to the pasta, tossing gently to mix. Return the pasta to the oven to keep warm.

- In the same skillet, adding more butter if necessary, sauté the chicken for about 5 minutes, or until the chicken is cooked and beginning to brown. Add the orange juice mixture to the skillet and cook for about 2 minutes longer, or until the mixture is bubbly and thick.

- Serve the chicken with orange sauce on top of or along-side the pasta. Garnish with green onions or chives and orange slices.

Remember important dates like birthdays and anniversaries.

Chicken-Basil-Blue Pasta

If you don't have a meat mallet, you can substitute a can from your pantry, a rolling pin, or even the bottom of a heavy glass.

2   skinless boneless chicken breasts

4   ounces radiatore (little radiators) pasta

1   teaspoon butter

¼   cup chopped oil-packed sun-dried tomatoes, drained, 2 tablespoons oil reserved

2   garlic cloves, minced

¼   cup chopped fresh basil

¼   cup canned chicken broth

¼   cup crumbled blue cheese, plus additional for garnish

    Salt and pepper to taste

Equipment
Meat mallet
Large saucepan
Medium bowl
Large skillet

Servings
2

Preparation Time
20 minutes

Total Time
20 minutes

- Rinse the chicken breasts under cold running water; drain. Place the chicken between sheets of plastic wrap, and with the flat side of a meat mallet, pound the chicken from the center out until it is approximately ¼-inch thick all around.

- In a large pot of boiling salted water cook the pasta until tender but still firm to bite. Drain and place in a medium bowl. Add the butter and toss until the butter melts and the pasta is coated. Keep the pasta warm in an oven set on low.

- Meanwhile, in a large skillet heat 1 tablespoon of the tomato oil over medium-high heat. Add the chicken breasts and sauté until cooked through, about 2 minutes per side.

- Remove the chicken from the skillet and let cool. Cut into ½-inch pieces.

- In the same skillet heat the remaining 1 tablespoon tomato oil over medium-high heat. Add the garlic, and sauté until softened but not browned, about 1 minute. Add the sun-dried tomatoes, chicken pieces, basil, and chicken broth. Let the mixture come to a boil. Reduce

When eating in front of the TV, sit back and snuggle until your program is over instead of immediately getting up to wash the dishes. This provides you with a little bit of relaxing downtime with your partner.

the heat to medium and simmer for 5 minutes. Remove from the heat and stir in the blue cheese until is is mostly melted.

- Pour the sauce over the cooked pasta and toss to coat. Season to taste with salt and pepper. Sprinkle with additional blue cheese for garnish, if desired.

Tell your partner three things you are thankful for.

Doc's Super-Secret Special Meat Sauce

Although we usually prefer spaghetti sauce made from scratch, there are some decent bottled varieties out there. Try Classico, Five Brothers, or Colavita. Keep a jar on hand for those times when you are just too tired to make your own sauce.

$\frac{1}{4}$ pound ground beef (10–15 percent fat)

$\frac{1}{4}$ cup water

1 teaspoon chili powder

Salt and pepper to taste

$1\frac{1}{2}$ cups of your favorite bottled or homemade marinara sauce

---

- In a large skillet combine the ground beef and water over low heat. Using a fork, whisk, or wooden spoon, stir and break up the meat until the water is incorporated. It will have a souplike consistency.

- Increase the heat to medium-high. Let the mixture come to a boil, and cook, stirring, until the beef is browned and the water has evaporated. The meat will be in very fine bits at this point.

- Add the chili powder and salt and pepper to taste. Pour in the marinara sauce and cook for about 5 minutes, until the sauce is heated through.

- Serve hot over freshly cooked pasta sprinkled with Parmesan cheese and dried crushed red pepper.

Note
To freeze sauce for later use, ladle approximately $\frac{3}{4}$ cup cooled sauce into quart-size plastic freezer bags, and store flat in freezer.

Equipment
Large skillet

Servings
2

Serving Suggestions
Serve over hot cooked pasta with Parmesan cheese and dried crushed red pepper.

Preparation Time
15 minutes

Total Time
20 minutes

Flattened Oven-Fried Chicken

If you don't have a meat mallet, you can substitute a can from your pantry, a rolling pin, or even the bottom of a heavy glass. Try the variation for chicken nuggets!

2	boneless skinless chicken breasts
1	egg white
1½	cups corn flakes, or ¾ cup breadcrumbs, or 16 saltine crackers
½	teaspoon garlic salt
¼	teaspoon pepper
½	teaspoon chili powder
1	tablespoon flour

- Preheat the oven to 350°F. Coat a baking sheet with vegetable oil spray.

- Rinse the chicken breasts under cold running water; drain. Place the chicken between sheets of plastic wrap, and with the flat side of a meat mallet, pound the chicken from the center out until it is approximately ¼-inch thick all around.

- In a shallow dish lightly beat the egg white. Place the flattened chicken breasts in the egg white, coating both sides.

- Crush the corn flakes, breadcrumbs, or saltines very finely with hands or a rolling pin in a large plastic zipper bag. Add the garlic salt, pepper, chili powder, and flour to the bag. Shake to mix well.

- Add the chicken breasts to the bag, and shake lightly. Be sure both sides are coated with crumbs.

- Place the chicken on the prepared baking sheet. Bake for 15 minutes or until the chicken is cooked through and the juices run clear.

- *Variation for chicken nuggets:* Do not pound the chicken flat. Cut the chicken into 1-inch chunks. Coat in egg white and crumbs, and bake as directed.

Equipment
Meat mallet
Shallow dish
Baking sheet

Servings
2

Serving Suggestions
- Baked French Fries (p. 159)
- Baked Onion Rings (p. 160)

Preparation Time
10 minutes

Total Time
25 minutes

Grandma's Yaki Soba

A Japanese recipe that we've adapted slightly to use ingredients easily found in American supermarkets. You can use olive oil instead of bacon for a vegetarian version; just be sure to season the yaki soba with extra salt and pepper.

4	ounces dried soba noodles
2	slices bacon, chopped
1	cup thinly sliced onion
4	cups shredded green cabbage
1	cup fresh bean sprouts
¼	cup Tonkatsu sauce (Japanese steak sauce), plus extra for serving

- In a large pot of boiling salted water cook the soba noodles until tender but still firm to bite. Drain and transfer to a medium bowl.

- Meanwhile, in an electric wok or large skillet over medium-high heat cook the bacon until it just begins to turn crisp.

- Add the onions to the skillet and sauté lightly until just translucent. Add the cabbage, noodles, and bean sprouts. Stir-fry for 5 to 10 minutes, until the cabbage is wilted and the mixture is heated through.

- Add ¼ cup Tonkatsu sauce and cook for about 2 more minutes.

- Remove from the heat and serve, passing extra Tonkatsu sauce.

Notes

Soba noodles are sold in the Asian food section of some supermarkets. They are very similar to the noodles that come in packages of ramen soup, and these can be substituted (without their seasoning packet) if necessary.

Tonkatsu sauce is sold in Asian food markets and in some large supermarkets. If you can't find it, you can approximate it by mixing ½ cup A-1 steak sauce with 1 tablespoon honey and 1 tablespoon applesauce.

Equipment

Electric wok or large skillet

Servings

2

Serving Suggestions

Try a Japanese beer with this dish. There are many excellent ones, some that are even brewed locally. Asahi, Sapporo, and Kirin are a few of the most popular Japanese ales.

Preparation Time

20 minutes

Total Time

20 minutes

Grilled Club Sandwich Wraps with Raspberry-Chipotle Sauce

You can roll pretty much anything into a tortilla and grill it, but this flavor combination is awesome. If you can't find raspberry-chipotle sauce, substitute honey-mustard dressing or your favorite sauce.

2	slices lean bacon
2	10-inch flour tortillas
¼	cup sliced green onions
4	ounces Havarti or Monterey Jack cheese, grated
4	ounces thinly sliced smoked turkey breast
1	cup lightly packed baby spinach leaves
1	small Roma tomato, chopped
4	tablespoons bottled raspberry-chipotle sauce, plus extra for dipping

- Place the bacon on a microwave-safe plate between double layers of paper towels. Microwave for 3 to 4 minutes, or until the bacon is crisp. Crumble the bacon into small pieces.

- Lay the tortillas flat on a clean counter and divide the green onions, cheese, turkey, bacon, spinach, and tomato evenly between them. Drizzle two tablespoons of raspberry-chipotle sauce over the filling in each tortilla, and loosely roll up. Gently press to flatten slightly.

- Spray a large skillet with vegetable oil spray, and place on medium-high heat. When hot, place one tortilla roll in the skillet seam side down. Toast until golden, turning to cook both sides, about 3 minutes.

- Repeat with the remaining tortilla, spraying the pan again with vegetable oil spray.

- Slice the hot rolls in half, securing each half with a toothpick, and serve with extra raspberry-chipotle sauce.

Equipment
Paper towels
Microwave-safe plate
Large skillet
Toothpicks

Servings
2

Serving Suggestions
- Potato chips
- Beer or soda

Preparation Time
15 minutes

Total Time
15 minutes

Yankee Fajitas

Also known as cheese-steak sandwiches! These are a bit different from the traditional in that we used Swiss cheese instead of Provolone, but substitute whichever cheese strikes your fancy. Pepper Jack could move these Yankee Fajitas south of the Mason-Dixon line! The green peppers are also optional, but we like a lot of 'em.

2	teaspoons vegetable oil
½	cup sliced green bell pepper
½	cup sliced red onion
¼	pound deli roast beef (lunchmeat slices), chopped
	Salt and pepper to taste
2	slices Swiss cheese
1	tablespoon mayonnaise
4	slices hearty Italian or sourdough bread

- In a large skillet heat the oil over medium-high heat. Add the bell pepper and onion and sauté until crisp-tender, about 5 minutes. Add the chopped roast beef, and sauté another 5 minutes. Season to taste with salt and pepper.

- Turn off the heat but leave the pan on the stove. Separate the mixture into 2 sections in the pan, and place a slice of cheese on each. Let sit for a few minutes, until the cheese melts.

- Spread the mayonnaise on two slices of bread and place on plates. With a large spatula or pancake turner, lift a section of the meat and place on the bread, and top with a slice of plain bread. Repeat with the remaining sandwich.

Equipment
Large skillet

Servings
2

Preparation Time
15 minutes

Total Time
20 minutes

Hot Turkey Sandwiches

This is kind of like a light version of the traditional cheesesteak, except without the cheese. And without the steak. You might call it a cheeseless cheeseturkey.

4	ounces deli turkey lunchmeat slices
1	tablespoon vegetable oil
½	cup onion, cut into strips
	Salt and pepper to taste
2	tablespoons mayonnaise
2	tablespoons yellow mustard
2	sandwich buns or hoagie rolls, split

- Stack the turkey slices together and cut them into ¼-inch strips. Cut the strips in half.

- In a skillet heat the oil over medium-high heat. When hot, add the onion and sauté for 2 minutes, until it is just beginning to turn translucent.

- Add the turkey to the skillet and cook an additional 5 minutes or so, stirring, until the turkey begins to brown. Season to taste with salt and pepper.

- Meanwhile, in a small bowl combine the mayonnaise and mustard. Toast the sandwich buns in a toaster oven or under the oven broiler until golden-brown and crisp.

- Spread both halves of the sandwich buns with the mayonnaise-mustard mixture. Pile half of the turkey mixture on each sandwich, add the top bun, and cut in half. Serve hot.

Note
Lunchmeat quality can vary greatly, so use the best you can find—have it sliced fresh at the deli counter. You could even use shredded cooked turkey breast in this recipe, but lunchmeat is fine if you have it on hand.

Equipment
Skillet
Small bowl

Servings
2

Preparation Time
10 minutes

Total Time
10 minutes

Picnic Chicken with Sesame-Citrus Sauce

We love taking this on picnics—it's great served cold or at room temperature. It can be a little messy, so be sure to pack plenty of napkins or wet wipes!

¼	cup orange juice
2	tablespoons lemon juice
1	tablespoon orange marmalade
1	tablespoon seasoned rice vinegar or white wine vinegar
	Grated rind of 1 small orange
1	teaspoon sesame oil
	Salt and cayenne pepper to taste
1	tablespoon sesame seeds
2	boneless chicken breast halves, with skin
1	tablespoon olive oil

• Preheat the oven to 400°F.

• In a small saucepan combine the orange and lemon juices, marmalade, vinegar, orange rind, sesame oil, salt, and cayenne pepper to taste, and heat over high heat until boiling. Reduce the heat and simmer for 5 minutes. Remove the sauce from the stove.

• Meanwhile, place the sesame seeds in a shallow dish. Sprinkle the chicken with salt and pepper. Coat the skin side of the chicken with seeds.

• In a large nonstick skillet heat the olive oil over high heat. Add the chicken, skin side down, and cook for approximately 3 minutes. Turn the chicken over and cook 3 minutes longer.

• Place the chicken, skin side up, into an 8-inch square or smaller baking dish. Pour half of the sauce over the chicken. Cover the dish with a lid or aluminum foil and bake in the oven about 20 minutes, or until the chicken is cooked through.

- Serve the chicken hot with the extra sauce. You can also let the chicken cool for about an hour, chill it and the reserved sauce overnight, and serve it cold or at room temperature.

Eat naked.
(Cooking naked is a safety hazard.)

Is microwaving romantic? It can be,
as long as you and your partner are
eating together with few distractions.

Quick Sliced Pork Sandwiches

These sandwiches are also great with Monterey Jack cheese. Try serving with bottled raspberry-chipotle sauce for a tangy twist.

2   4-ounce boneless pork cutlets ($\frac{1}{2}$-inch thick)
2   teaspoons vegetable oil
2   tablespoons soy sauce
    Lemon pepper to taste
2   wheat or white sub rolls or sandwich buns

Equipment
Skillet
Meat mallet

Servings
2

Preparation Time
15 minutes

Total Time
15 minutes

- Trim any visible fat from the pork cutlets. Place the cutlets in a plastic zipper bag or on a cutting board under a sheet of plastic wrap and pound with a meat mallet or rolling pin until $\frac{1}{4}$-inch thick.

- In a skillet heat the oil over medium-high heat. When hot, place the flattened pork cutlets in the skillet and sprinkle with 1 tablespoon soy sauce and lemon pepper. Let cook for 3 to 4 minutes, then turn over.

- Pour the remaining 1 tablespoon soy sauce over the pork, and sprinkle with lemon pepper. Let cook for another 3 to 4 minutes, or until cooked through and nicely browned.

- Remove from the pan and slice into $\frac{1}{4}$-inch slices.

- Meanwhile, toast the sandwich buns in a toaster oven or under the oven broiler until golden-brown and crisp.

- Arrange the pork on the sandwiches, cut in half, and serve.

Lemon Herb Chicken

A very simple marinated baked chicken. Herbs de Provence is a spice mixture from the South of France, usually containing thyme, basil, savory, fennel, and lavender—but you can use any herbs that you like in the marinade.

¼	cup lemon juice
¼	teaspoon garlic salt
¼	teaspoon pepper
1	teaspoon crushed herbs de Provence (or other herbs of choice)
2	boneless skinless chicken breast halves

- In a small bowl combine the lemon juice, garlic salt, pepper, and herbs de Provence. Add the chicken to the bowl and turn to coat. Marinate for 30 minutes to 1 hour.

- Preheat the oven to 400°F. Lightly oil a baking sheet.

- Place the chicken on the prepared baking sheet. Bake the chicken for 25 minutes, or until the chicken is cooked through and the juices run clear.

Equipment
Small bowl
Baking sheet

Servings
2

Serving Suggestions
- Baked potato or garlic bread
- White zinfandel wine

Preparation Time
5 minutes

Total Time
1 hour

Leftover Chicken Pesto Pizza

Leftover chicken? No problem! This is a great way to use it up. The taste of the pesto and tomato paste together is unbeatable, and the pizza can be made with any conceivable combination of toppings. The only constants should be the chicken, pesto, tomato paste, and cheese. Try with artichoke hearts and thinly sliced tomatoes, or Monterey Jack cheese instead of Mozzarella.

Equipment
Pizza stone or baking sheet

Servings
4

Serving Suggestions
• Pizza is great with dipping sauces—try ranch dressing or marinara sauce.
• Serve with a tossed green salad or Fast Fresh Fruit Salad (p. 141)

Preparation Time
10 minutes

Total Time
25 minutes

1	12-inch pre-baked pizza crust (try Katy's Grilled Pizza Crusts, p. 68)
	Olive oil
3	large cloves garlic, minced
3	tablespoons pesto (storebought is fine)
1/4	cup tomato paste
1	tablespoon dried oregano leaves
1	teaspoon garlic salt
1	leftover baked or grilled chicken breast (try Flattened Oven-Fried Chicken, p. 91)
1	small Roma tomato, diced
1/4	cup sliced green olives
1	stalk green onion, thinly sliced
3	tablespoons freshly grated Parmesan cheese
1	cup grated Mozzarella cheese
	Coarse cornmeal

• Preheat the oven and pizza stone or baking sheet to 500°F.

• Brush the pizza crust lightly with olive oil. Sprinkle the minced garlic evenly over the crust. Using a rubber spatula or the back of a spoon, spread the pesto over the crust and garlic. Spread the tomato paste on top of the pesto (it will get mixed in). Sprinkle the oregano and garlic salt on top.

• Slice the leftover chicken breast thinly and cut into ½-inch pieces. Place evenly atop the crust. Add the tomato, olives, and onion. Sprinkle evenly with Parmesan and Mozzarella cheeses.

Go grocery shopping together.

- Remove the hot pizza stone or baking sheet from the oven, and sprinkle the surface with a thin layer of cornmeal. Place the pizza on top of the cornmeal. This will prevent the pizza crust from sticking.

- Reduce the heat to 425°F, and bake for about 15 minutes or until the cheese is melted and beginning to brown.

Eat at the dining table and not in front of the TV.

Doc's Bierocks

Bierocks are buns stuffed with a savory beef filling. They are very popular in Kansas. We normally don't recommend using prepared bread products like the refrigerated can of rolls, but it works well for convenience's sake. If you have the time, by all means make your own bread dough for these.

Equipment
Large skillet
Baking sheet

Servings
4

Serving Suggestions
These are great with beer.

Preparation Time
40 minutes

Total Time
1 hour

½	pound ground beef (85 percent fat)
¼	cup water
½	teaspoon salt
½	teaspoon pepper
1¼	cups finely chopped yellow onion
¼	small head green cabbage, finely shredded (about 4 cups)
1	large can refrigerated dinner rolls (8 rolls)

• In a large skillet combine the ground beef and water. Using a fork, whisk, or wooden spoon, stir and break up the meat until the water is incorporated. It will have a souplike consistency.

• Put the skillet on the stove over medium-high heat. Let the mixture come to a boil, and cook, stirring, for about 15 minutes or until the beef is browned and the water has evaporated. The meat will be in very fine bits at this point. Pour off any excess water, if necessary, holding the meat back with a slotted spoon or strainer. Season with salt and pepper.

• Add the onions and cabbage to the skillet, and continue cooking until the onions are translucent and the cabbage has wilted, about 10 minutes. Let the mixture cool completely in the refrigerator or freezer, stirring occasionally to let off heat.

• Preheat the oven to 375°F.

Dress up for dinner.

- Separate the dinner roll dough, and with a rolling pin roll it out into 6-inch circles. Place about ⅓ cup filling into the center of each circle, and bring up the edges to the center. Pinch to seal tightly.

- Place the bierocks, seam side down, on an ungreased baking sheet. Bake for 25 minutes, or until the tops are golden brown.

Make a romantic meal for Mom and Dad, and
deliver it with candles and a bottle of wine,
kind of like a romantic Meals on Wheels.

Husband Pleasin' Hamburger Casserole

Katy adapted this casserole from a 1970s-era cookbook, compiled by the ladies at the hospital where her Grandma Ruby volunteered. Similar to lasagna, it's a great meal for cold weather and it makes the house smell wonderful.

½   pound ground sirloin beef or turkey (10 percent fat or less)
½   teaspoon garlic salt
½   teaspoon onion salt
    Pepper to taste
½   teaspoon sugar
1   15-ounce can tomato sauce
4   ounces rotini (spiral) pasta
2   ounces light (or regular) cream cheese
½   cup light (or regular) sour cream
    Garlic salt to taste
½   cup grated low fat (or regular) Cheddar cheese

• Preheat the oven to 350°F. Grease a small glass baking dish.

• In a large skillet cook the ground beef over medium-high heat until it is browned and cooked through. Crumble it up into small pieces with the back of a wooden spoon while it is cooking.

• When the beef is nicely browned, pour off the grease into an empty metal can by holding the beef back with a slotted spoon or strainer. Return the skillet to the stove. Add the garlic salt, onion salt, pepper, sugar, and tomato sauce to the skillet. Cover and simmer on medium heat for 15 minutes.

• Meanwhile, in a large pot of boiling salted water cook the pasta until tender but still firm to bite. Drain.

Equipment
Large skillet
Large pot
Small bowl
Small glass baking dish

Serving Suggestions
• Green salad
• Garlic bread
• White wine

Servings
4

Preparation Time
30 minutes

Total Time
1 hour

Plan your dream vacation.

- In a small bowl combine the cream cheese and sour cream. Add the garlic salt to taste.

- In the prepared baking dish make two layers each of the pasta, the meat sauce, and the sour cream mixture. Sprinkle the top with Cheddar cheese.

- Bake for 30 minutes, until the cheese is melted and the casserole is bubbly. Let stand for 10 minutes before serving.

Tell your partner you love them at least once a day.

Serve hot apple cider or hot chocolate on a cold night.

Equipment
Large pot
Cheese grater or food
   processor

Serving Suggestions
Chili practically MUST be
served with saltine crackers. It is also tradition in
Katy's family to add a
squirt of yellow mustard
on top—but without the
cheese.

Servings
6

Preparation Time
15 minutes

Total Time
3 hours 15 minutes

Weekend Chili

*It's called "Weekend Chili" because you can just throw the ingredients
into a big pot and let it simmer all afternoon. It makes about six servings,
so you will have leftovers to take to work the next week!*

1	tablespoon olive oil
4	ounces ground sirloin beef (optional)
1	large yellow onion, diced
3	large cloves garlic, minced
1	15-ounce can chili beans (or pinto beans)
1	15-ounce can Great Northern (white) beans
2	14-ounce cans diced tomatoes
1	6-ounce can spicy V8 juice (or 6 ounces tomato juice)
3	large carrots
¾	cup frozen corn kernels
1	medium green bell pepper, diced
2	tablespoons chili powder
1	tablespoon ground cumin
1	tablespoon oregano
1	teaspoon thyme
2	teaspoons salt
2	teaspoons sugar
	Salt and pepper to taste
	Tabasco sauce to taste
1	cup grated Monterey Jack cheese (optional)

- In a large pot heat the olive oil on medium heat. If
  using the ground beef, stir it in the pot until browned.

- Add the onion and garlic and cook, stirring, for about
  5 minutes or until the onion begins to turn translucent.

- Reduce the heat to low. Add the chili beans and their
  juices, Great Northern beans and their juices, tomatoes
  and their juices, and V8 juice. Cover and let simmer
  while you prepare the vegetables.

- Peel the carrots and shred them with a food processor or the large holes of a cheese grater. Add them to the pot along with the corn and the diced bell pepper. Stir in the chili powder, cumin, oregano, thyme, salt, and sugar.

- Let the chili simmer, covered, over low heat for about three hours, stirring occasionally.

- Add the salt, pepper, and Tabasco sauce to taste, and ladle the chili into serving bowls. Top with shredded Monterey Jack cheese if desired.

Being surprised by exotic foods that you can't easily get (Turkish Delight, tropical fruit, European chocolates) can be very romantic.

On a cold night, eat in your favorite snuggly robe.

Equipment
Large pot
Small saucepan

Servings
2

Serving Suggestions
• Green salad with vinai-
  grette
• The richness of this
  dish requires some
  sort of flavorful bever-
  age as a counterpoint.
  Although cream sauces
  are most often paired
  with a white wine, the
  sharpness of this
  recipe can even take a
  rich red wine like
  Chianti.

Preparation Time
10 minutes

Total Time
15 minutes

Arushi's Gorgonzola Alfredo

This is super-fast, super-rich, super-creamy, and very gourmet. It was a method that Arushi's house-mom used while she was living in Salzburg, Austria.

6	ounces linguine pasta
4	ounces Gorgonzola cheese (a mild Italian blue cheese)
½	cup heavy (whipping) cream
	Salt and pepper to taste

• In a large pot of boiling salted water cook the linguine until tender but still firm to bite. Drain.

• Meanwhile, in a small saucepan heat the Gorgonzola cheese over medium heat. Stir the cheese constantly until melted, about 5 to 7 minutes.

• Stir in the heavy cream until blended and heated through, but not boiling. Add the salt and pepper to taste.

• Divide the pasta between two serving bowls and pour the sauce on top. Serve hot.

Flaming desserts are romantic, sometimes. Just don't burn yourself.

Black Bean Burritos

2	10-inch flour tortillas
1	teaspoon oil
¼	cup chopped onion
¼	teaspoon ground cumin
¼	teaspoon chili powder
¾	cup canned black beans, rinsed and drained
¼	cup diced tomatoes
1	teaspoon minced seeded jalapeño
	Salt and pepper to taste
4	tablespoons grated Monterey Jack cheese
2	tablespoons sour cream
2	tablespoons chopped fresh cilantro

Equipment
Aluminum foil
Medium skillet

Servings
2

Serving Suggestions
• Tortilla chips, salsa, and queso
• Mexican beer such as Corona

Preparation Time
15 minutes

Total Time
20 minutes

- Preheat the oven to 350°F. Wrap the tortillas in foil and warm in the oven until heated through, about 15 minutes.

- Meanwhile, in a skillet heat the oil over medium-high heat. Sauté the onion until golden and translucent, about 6 minutes. Add the cumin, chili powder, black beans, tomatoes, and jalapeño. Bring to a simmer and let cook for about 5 minutes. Season with salt and pepper. Remove from the heat.

- Place the warm tortillas on a work surface. Spoon the black beans down the center, dividing equally. Top each with 2 tablespoons Monterey Jack cheese, 1 tablespoon sour cream, and 1 tablespoon cilantro. Fold the end of the tortilla up and then fold the sides over the filling, forming packages. Turn seam side down onto plate.

- Serve hot with extra sour cream, cilantro, and salsa.

Breakfast Tortillas

This was standard breakfast fare in Katy's house for many years. The tortillas can be served for any meal, but it does make for a very filling and easily prepared breakfast before work or school. Plus, it is high in both protein and carbohydrates.

2	6- or 7-inch flour tortillas
⅔	cup fat-free refried beans
½	cup grated Cheddar or Pepper Jack cheese, loosely packed
1	teaspoon butter
2	eggs
	Salt and pepper to taste
	Salsa (optional)

Equipment
Microwave
Medium skillet

Serving Suggestions
Great with a cold glass of orange juice.

Servings
2

Preparation Time
5 minutes

Total Time
5 minutes

- Spread each tortilla with half of the refried beans and sprinkle with half of the cheese. Season to taste with salt and pepper.

- Place the tortillas on microwave-safe plates and cover loosely with plastic wrap or waxed paper (beans in the microwave tend to explode). Microwave 2 to 3 minutes on high, until the cheese melts and is bubbly.

- Meanwhile, in a medium skillet melt the butter. Cook the eggs sunny-side up, over easy, or scrambled. When done, place one egg on top of each tortilla. Serve hot with salsa on the side, if desired.

Serve your partner breakfast in bed. Or dinner in bed.

Cheddar Fondue

Fondue was a special Friday night tradition when Katy was growing up. Her parents would haul the little black and white television set into the kitchen and they'd watch TV while eating. This is probably part of the reason she has such a special fondness for, or should we say addiction to, cheese today.

1	tablespoon dry mustard powder
2	tablespoons water
3	tablespoons butter
3	tablespoons flour
¼	teaspoon pepper
½	teaspoon salt
1	cup milk
2	cups grated sharp Cheddar cheese
	Cubed French bread
	Diced vegetables and fruit

- In a small bowl mix the dry mustard with the water, and set aside.

- If you have a fondue pot, light its fuel canister (Sterno) on high. If you don't have a fondue pot, you can use a double boiler on the stove. Get some water boiling in the lower pot, and then set the upper pot in place.

- Melt the butter in the pot. With a whisk, gradually stir in the flour, pepper, and salt. Slowly whisk in the milk, just a bit at a time, stirring until smooth.

- Add the Cheddar cheese by the handful, stirring with a spoon until melted. Once all the cheese is melted, add the mustard mixture. Blend the fondue well.

- Season to taste with additional salt and pepper, if needed. Serve hot with chunks of French bread, fruit, and vegetables for dipping.

Note
There are several different varieties of fondue: the standard cheese version, the classic hot oil or broth into which meat and vegetables are dipped and cooked, and the luscious dessert fondues, most often made of chocolate (p. 182) or caramel and accompanied by chunks of angel food cake, maraschino cherries, and fruit.

Equipment
Small bowl
Fondue pot or double
  boiler

Serving Suggestions
Cheese fondue's classic accompaniment is cubed French bread. However, we also love to use chunks of tart green apple, carrot, cauliflower, broccoli, pear, mushroom caps, and other types of bread such as rye or herbed sourdough.
   Fondue is an excellent opportunity to break out your hidden cups and bowls, especially fun mismatched ones, to fill with the breads and vegetables.

Servings
2 to 3

Preparation Time
15 minutes

Total Time
15 minutes

Confetti Rice Salad

Equipment
Medium saucepan
Large bowl
Small bowl

Servings
4

Preparation Time
15 minutes

Total Time
40 minutes

1	cup rice
2	cups water
1	cup corn kernels (canned or frozen)
1	small carrot, peeled and grated
1	small jalapeño pepper, seeded and diced
¼	cup chopped green olives
½	cup chopped yellow bell pepper
½	cup chopped red bell pepper
½	cup sliced green onions
2	ounces Pepper Jack cheese, cut into ¼-inch cubes
½	teaspoon crushed red pepper
5	teaspoons lime juice
1½	teaspoons white wine vinegar
1½	teaspoons olive oil
½	teaspoon minced garlic
¼	teaspoon sugar
	Salt and pepper to taste

- In a medium saucepan combine the rice and water, and bring to a boil over high heat. Reduce the heat to medium-low, cover the pot, and let the rice simmer until it is cooked through and all the water is absorbed, about 15 to 20 minutes. Don't stir the rice or lift the lid while it is cooking.

- Let the rice cool in the refrigerator or freezer to room temperature or slightly chilled, stirring occasionally to release the heat.

- Meanwhile, in a large bowl stir together the corn, grated carrot, jalapeño pepper, olives, bell peppers, green onions, cheese, and crushed red pepper until well mixed. Stir in the cooled rice.

- In a small bowl whisk the lime juice with vinegar, oil, garlic, and sugar. Season to taste with salt and pepper. Pour over the rice mixture, and toss to coat.

- Serve chilled or at room temperature.

Creamy Mushroom Linguine

This is a lighter vegetarian version of the classic beef stroganoff.

4	ounces linguine pasta
1	teaspoon butter
2	teaspoons olive oil
1	small onion, thinly sliced
1	clove garlic, minced
1	pound mushrooms, sliced
2	teaspoons flour
1/8	teaspoon ground nutmeg
1/4	cup white wine
1/2	cup light sour cream
	Salt and pepper to taste

- In a large pot of boiling salted water cook the linguine until tender but still firm to bite. Drain and place in a medium bowl. Add 1 teaspoon butter and toss until the butter melts and the pasta is coated. Keep the pasta warm in an oven set on low.

- Meanwhile, in a large skillet heat the olive oil on medium-high heat. Add the onions, garlic, and mushrooms. Sauté until the onions are translucent, most of the liquid has evaporated, and the mushrooms have begun to brown, about 10 minutes.

- Reduce the heat to medium. Sprinkle the flour and nutmeg over the mushroom mixture and stir for 1 minute. Add the wine and cook until the mixture thickens, stirring frequently, about 3 minutes.

- Mix in the sour cream and season to taste with salt and pepper. Pour the mushroom sauce over the warm pasta and toss lightly to coat. Serve immediately.

Equipment
Large pot
Medium bowl
Large skillet

Servings
2

Serving Suggestions
- Add sliced grilled chicken breast for some added protein.
- Sautéed Green Beans (p. 166)

Preparation Time
20 minutes

Total Time
20 minutes

Ratatouille

Ratatouille is a fancy term for a very healthy, very fresh, and very fast squash stew. Chop the vegetables first to save time.

1 tablespoon olive oil
2 cloves garlic, minced
1 small yellow squash, diced
1 small zucchini, diced
1 tablespoon dried basil
1 tablespoon dried oregano
1 14-ounce can whole tomatoes, undrained
   Salt and pepper to taste

- In a large saucepan heat the olive oil on medium-high heat. Add the garlic, yellow squash, and zucchini. Cook until the vegetables soften, stirring frequently, about 5 minutes. Add the basil, oregano, and canned tomatoes with their liquid. Add salt and pepper to taste.

- Cover the pan and cook for 15 to 20 minutes, until the vegetables become almost stew-like.

- Ladle into soup bowls and serve.

Feed each other fresh strawberries.

Variation

Add your favorite leftover cooked meat to the last stage of cooking. The meat will become tender and pick up the flavor of the vegetables and spices. Or serve the ratatouille over your favorite pasta. Angel hair pasta, is, as always, the fastest choice.

Equipment
Large saucepan

Servings
2

Serving Suggestions
- Dinner rolls or garlic bread
- Merlot or Cabernet Sauvignon wine

Preparation Time
10 minutes

Total Time
25 minutes

Easy Salsa Pasta

This can be as mild or as spicy as you like, depending on the type of salsa you use. Try melting some Velveeta into the salsa mixture and reducing the amount of Cheddar you sprinkle on top. You could also add some chopped cooked chicken to the dish.

4	ounces small shell pasta
½	cup canned corn or frozen corn, thawed
¼	cup green bell pepper, chopped
½	cup of your favorite salsa (try Katy's Hot Salsa, p. 157)
½	of a 15-ounce can diced tomatoes with juices (about 1 cup)
½	teaspoon ground cumin
½	teaspoon chili powder
	Salt and pepper to taste
½	cup shredded Cheddar cheese

- In a large pot of boiling salted water cook the shell pasta until tender but still firm to bite. Drain.

- Meanwhile, in a medium saucepan heat the corn, bell pepper, salsa, and tomatoes to boiling. Reduce the heat to low; add the cumin and chili powder. Simmer, uncovered, for about 5 minutes. Add salt and pepper to taste.

- Preheat the broiler.

- Stir the pasta into the sauce. Transfer the mixture to a 8-inch square glass baking dish, and sprinkle with cheese. Broil, uncovered, for a few minutes until the cheese melts and is bubbly.

- Serve hot.

Equipment
Large pot
Medium saucepan
8-inch-square glass baking dish

Servings
2

Serving Suggestions
Magical Southwestern Black Beans (p. 118)

Preparation Time
15 minutes

Total Time
20 minutes

Hearty Grilled Tofu

Leftover grilled tofu is a great way to add protein to a pasta salad. Simply cut the tofu into small cubes and add to Festival Pasta Salad, p. 134.

1	14-ounce package baked tofu (see note)
4	tablespoons olive oil
	Salt and pepper to taste
4	tablespoons lemon juice

- Preheat the barbecue grill to medium-hot.

- Remove the tofu from the package and rinse each square. Poke numerous small holes in each square with a fork.

- Place the tofu in a zipper bag with 2 tablespoons of olive oil. Shake until coated. Season to taste with salt and pepper.

- In a small bowl mix the lemon juice with the remaining 2 tablespoons olive oil. Season to taste with salt and pepper.

- Place the tofu on the hot grill and baste with the lemon juice mixture. Grill the tofu for about 3 to 4 minutes per side, basting regularly, until it is nicely browned and beginning to char and bubble.

- Remove from the grill and serve hot.

Turn off the TV while eating.

Note
Baked tofu is available in the refrigerated section of some Asian food markets. It comes in the form of flattened 2-inch squares and is extremely firm and compact. Unlike regular tofu, which is smooth and soft, the texture is dense, springy, and almost cheese-like. If you can't find baked tofu, you can use extra-firm regular tofu, pressed and drained, but the texture will be different.

Equipment
Barbecue grill
Small bowl

Servings
4

Serving Suggestions
- Steamed white rice or garlic bread
- Grilled Vegetables (p. 170)
- A-1 Sauce

Preparation Time
15 minutes

Total Time
15 minutes

Katy's Garlic Mushroom Red Sauce

This sauce makes a large quantity, and it freezes well so you can always have some on hand. As a variation, try cooking 1 pound of crumbled ground beef before adding the onions and garlic. Also great with ½ cup sliced Kalamata olives.

1	tablespoon oil
1	large onion, diced
8	cloves garlic, minced
½	cup red wine
1	12-ounce can tomato paste
1	28-ounce can diced tomatoes, undrained
1	28-ounce can crushed tomatoes, undrained
8	ounces mushrooms, rinsed, trimmed, and sliced
2	teaspoons balsamic vinegar
1	teaspoon honey
1	teaspoon dried oregano (or 1 tablespoon chopped fresh)
1	tablespoon dried basil (or 3 tablespoons chopped fresh)
	Salt and pepper to taste
	Accént or MSG to taste (optional)

- In a large nonstick pot heat the oil over medium heat. Add the onions and garlic. Sauté until the onions are tender and translucent, about 5 minutes.

- Add the red wine and tomato paste. Stir until well blended. Add the diced and crushed tomatoes with their juices, mushrooms, balsamic vinegar, honey, oregano, and basil. Season to taste with salt, pepper, and MSG, if desired.

- Reduce the heat to medium-low, and simmer the sauce, covered, stirring occasionally, for about 30 minutes.

- Serve hot over freshly cooked pasta sprinkled with Parmesan cheese and dried crushed red pepper.

Note
To freeze the sauce for later use, ladle approximately 1 cup cooled sauce into quart-size plastic freezer bags, and store them flat in the freezer.

Equipment
Large saucepan

Servings
8 to 10

Serving Suggestions
- Tossed green salad and vinaigrette dressing
- Garlic bread
- Chardonnay or Chablis wine

Preparation Time
10 minutes

Total Time
40 minutes

Magical Southwestern Black Beans

Black beans are one of the most nutritious foods on earth—high in protein and fiber and very filling. This dish is almost limitless in its adaptability. You can add as few or as many vegetables and hot peppers as you like.

2	tablespoons vegetable oil
3	cloves garlic, minced
1	jalapeño or serrano pepper, chopped (optional)
1	small onion, chopped
1	large tomato, chopped
1	15-ounce can black beans
1	tablespoon freshly squeezed lime juice
2	teaspoons salt
1/4	cup cilantro, chopped, for garnish
	Corn or flour tortillas

- In a heavy saucepan heat the oil on medium-high heat. Add the garlic and jalapeño or serrano pepper (if you are using it). Stand back, as the pan will get lively and pungent. Let it cook, stirring, for about a minute, but don't let it overheat, or it will burn.

- Add the chopped onions and tomatoes. Let them cook until softened, stirring often, at least 5 minutes. Reduce the heat to medium.

- Pour the black beans into a strainer and rinse them thoroughly. Drain the water from the beans, and add them to the pot. Cook until the beans are hot and simmering, about 5 to 10 minutes longer.

- Add the lime juice and salt, and garnish with the chopped cilantro. Serve with corn or flour tortillas.

Notes

The secret to this recipe is finding a brand of beans that you like. We use Eden Soy's Organic Black Beans, but you will likely settle on your own favorite.

Equipment

Heavy saucepan
Strainer

Servings

2

Serving Suggestions

- Serve this with plain sparkling water. The bubbles intensify the flavors.
- Serve with corn or flour tortillas. The beans can be rolled like an enchilada or eaten with the tortillas on the side. You can also sprinkle on cheese or add fresh guacamole (try Speedy Guacamole, p. 59). They also go well with lots of spicy salsa (try Katy's Hot Salsa, p. 157) or a scoop of fresh sour cream.

Preparation Time

15 minutes

Total Time

15 minutes

Portobello Mushroom Cap Pizzas

This is a good recipe for people who are watching their carbohydrate intake. Portobellos are meaty and hearty and make an unusual and tasty base for a pizza.

2	large portobello mushrooms
4	tablespoons tomato paste
1	teaspoon Italian seasoning (or use thyme, basil, or oregano)
	Salt and pepper to taste
¼	cup green bell pepper, finely diced
¼	cup onion, thinly sliced
½	cup grated Mozzarella cheese
2	tablespoons grated Parmesan cheese

- Preheat a baking sheet in the oven at 425°F.

- Briefly rinse the mushrooms under cold running water and pat dry. Trim the ends of the stems. Carefully cut the remaining stems out of the mushrooms and set aside.

- Spread two tablespoons tomato paste on the ridged underside of each mushroom cap. Sprinkle with Italian seasoning and salt and pepper to taste.

- Chop the reserved mushroom stems. In a small bowl toss the stems with the green peppers and onions. Sprinkle this mixture over the mushroom caps. Top with the Mozzarella and Parmesan cheeses.

- Carefully spray the preheated baking sheet with vegetable oil spray. Place the mushroom caps on the baking sheet and bake for about 8 to 10 minutes, or until the cheese has melted.

- Change the oven temperature to broil, and move the baking sheet to the top rack. Broil for a few minutes or until the cheese is bubbly and begins to brown. Be sure to watch very carefully because it can go from perfect to burnt in a matter of seconds.

- Remove from the oven and serve hot.

Equipment
Baking sheet
Small bowl

Servings
2

Serving Suggestions
- You could substitute pesto for the tomato paste, and sprinkle crumbled goat cheese instead of Mozzarella.
- Try adding pepperoni or Italian sausage to the vegetable mix to please meat lovers.

Preparation Time
10 minutes

Total Time
20 minutes

Potato Cakes with Tangy Apricot Sauce

When frying foods in oil, keep a small bowl of white vinegar sitting nearby to cut down on the smell.

Equipment
Small saucepan
Medium saucepan
Medium bowl
Medium skillet

Servings
2

Preparation Time
20 minutes

Total Time
30 minutes

1	small baking potato, peeled and cut into ½-inch chunks
½	cup apricot jam
1	tablespoon spicy brown mustard
½	teaspoon Tabasco sauce
¼	teaspoon sesame oil
1	teaspoon soy sauce
	Salt and pepper to taste
1	cup chickpeas (garbanzo beans), rinsed and drained (about half of a 15-ounce can)
1	teaspoon flour
½	teaspoon pepper
¼	teaspoon salt
	Dash nutmeg
¼	teaspoon dried oregano
1	clove garlic, minced
2	tablespoons thinly sliced green onions
2	teaspoons olive oil (more if necessary)

- Bring a medium saucepan of water to a boil over high heat. Add the potato chunks and boil until tender, about 10 minutes. Drain the potatoes and place them in a medium bowl.

- Meanwhile, in a small saucepan combine the apricot jam, mustard, Tabasco, sesame oil, soy sauce, and salt and pepper to taste over medium heat and simmer for 5 minutes, stirring occasionally. Remove from the heat and let cool.

- Add the chickpeas to the potatoes, and mash with a fork until mostly smooth with just a few lumps (or use a food processor to blend). Add the flour, pepper, salt, nutmeg, oregano, garlic, and green onions, and mix

Go out to dinner occasionally.

well. Form the potato mixture into flattened 2-inch patties, about $\frac{1}{2}$-inch thick.

- In a medium skillet heat the olive oil over medium-high heat. Working in batches, cook the potato cakes until light brown, about 3 minutes per side. Add more oil if necessary when cooking the remaining cakes.

- Serve hot with apricot sauce.

Make sure you say you like the dinner. Don't say your mother makes it better, even if it's true. Otherwise you may eat all of your meals alone.

Practically Immediate Baked Potatoes

If you don't have a steamer insert, you can use a regular saucepan. Fill it about halfway with water, and rest a wire mesh splatter screen or small wire strainer on top. Place the broccoli on the screen or in the strainer, cover with the saucepan lid, and let steam as directed. The idea is to suspend the broccoli in the steam from the pan. This technique can be used to steam almost any vegetable.

2	medium baking potatoes (such as Idaho russets)
1/2	cup frozen peas-and-carrots mix
1/2	cup small fresh broccoli florets
2	to 4 tablespoons chicken broth
2	tablespoons butter
1/4	cup sliced green onions or chives
	Salt and pepper to taste

Equipment
Waxed paper
Saucepan with steamer insert

Servings
2

Serving Suggestions
- Baked potatoes are really a meal unto themselves, and serving them this way is no exception. If you like meat, you could serve a grilled chicken breast or pork chop too.
- Potatoes can be served with any topping you can think of. The classic way is butter, sour cream, cheese, chives, and bacon bits.

Preparation Time
15 minutes

Total Time
15 minutes

- Scrub and rinse the potatoes well. Stab each potato all over with a fork 10 or 12 times, and wrap securely in a sheet of waxed paper.

- Microwave the potatoes on a microwave-safe plate for 8 to 10 minutes on high, or until the potatoes are cooked all the way through. You may need to adjust this cooking time, since microwave ovens vary in how quickly they cook.

- Meanwhile, in a saucepan with a steamer insert bring several inches of water to a boil (fill to just under the bottom of the steamer).

- Add the frozen peas-and-carrots mix to the boiling water. Place the steamer insert on top, add the broccoli to the steamer, and steam, covered, for about 5 minutes, until the broccoli is crisp-tender but still bright green. Remove from the heat. Drain the peas and carrots.

- When the potatoes are done, place them on serving plates, split open, and partially mash the insides, adding chicken broth to make them smooth. Top with peas and carrots, broccoli, butter, and green onions. Salt and pepper to taste.

Summer Tomato Pasta

This is one of the simplest dishes in this book—and can be prepared in about five minutes! It's also very healthy.

6	ounces angel hair pasta
1	teaspoon butter
2	medium tomatoes, chopped
2	cloves garlic, minced
1	teaspoon dried oregano leaves
¼	cup white wine
	Salt and pepper to taste
	Parmesan cheese

- In a large pot of boiling salted water cook the pasta until tender but still firm to bite. Angel hair cooks fast, so taste it every minute or so until it is done. Drain and place in a medium bowl. Add 1 teaspoon butter and toss until the butter melts and the pasta is coated. Keep the pasta warm in an oven set on low.

- Meanwhile, in a medium saucepan heat the chopped tomatoes, garlic, oregano, and white wine over medium-high heat. Bring to a boil and reduce the heat to low. Simmer for about 3 minutes. Remove from the heat and add salt and pepper to taste.

- Divide the pasta between two serving bowls or plates. Pour the tomato sauce over and sprinkle with Parmesan cheese.

Equipment
Large saucepan
Medium saucepan

Servings
2

Serving Suggestions
- Garlic bread
- Tossed salad
- White Zinfandel or Riesling wine

Preparation Time
5 minutes

Total Time
5 minutes

Spicy Spinach Angel Hair

This is also very good with tofu added for protein. Katy's favorite is baked pressed tofu from the Asian market, but you can use extra-firm regular tofu as well. Just dice it and add it with the onions and garlic.

6	ounces angel hair pasta
1	teaspoon butter
1	teaspoon olive oil
1	small yellow onion, diced
2	large cloves garlic, minced
1	cup chopped mushrooms
1	small fresh jalapeño pepper, seeded and sliced (adjust amount to taste)
¼	cup Sherry cooking wine
	Salt and pepper to taste
2	cups (packed) fresh spinach leaves, rinsed, patted dry, and chopped
½	cup grated Cheddar or Monterey Jack cheese, optional

- In a large pot of boiling salted water cook the pasta until tender but still firm to bite. Angel hair cooks fast, so taste it every minute or so until it is done. Drain and place in a medium bowl. Add 1 teaspoon butter and toss until the butter melts and the pasta is coated. Keep the pasta warm in an oven set on low.

- Meanwhile, in a large skillet heat the oil over medium-high heat. Add the onions and garlic and cook for about 3 minutes, stirring. Add the mushrooms and jalapeño. Cook for another 3 to 4 minutes, or until mushrooms have softened and the onion has turned translucent.

- Add the Sherry to the skillet and stir for a few minutes until most of the liquid has evaporated. Add the salt and pepper to taste.

Equipment
Large pot
Medium bowl
Large skillet with lid (or dinner plate as a lid substitute)

Servings
2

Serving Suggestions
- White wine
- A grilled chicken breast or pork cutlet, if you want some meat with your meal

Preparation Time
15 minutes

Total Time
15 minutes

*Make pancakes in the shape of hearts, and
top them with ice cream and maple syrup.*

- Add the chopped spinach leaves to the skillet and cover with a lid (or a dinner plate if your skillet has no lid). Let the spinach steam for about 3 minutes, then uncover and stir to mix. Remove from the heat.

- Divide the pasta between two serving bowls or plates. Top with spinach mixture, and sprinkle grated cheese on top.

*Use fun, mismatched plates, bowls,
and glasses.*

Tomato-Brie Pasta

4   ounces shell, rotini, or bow-tie pasta
1   14-ounce can diced tomatoes, drained
2   tablespoons wine or chicken broth
1   teaspoon dried basil
1   teaspoon dried oregano
1   teaspoon garlic salt
4   ounces Brie cheese
     Salt and pepper to taste
     Fresh basil, chopped (garnish)
     Kalamata olives (garnish)

- In a large pot of boiling salted water cook the pasta until tender but still firm to bite. Drain.

- Meanwhile, with a sharp knife cut the rind away from the Brie cheese. This is most easily done when the cheese is chilled and firm. Dice the Brie into cubes.

- In a medium saucepan heat the drained tomatoes and wine or chicken broth to boiling. Stir in the dried basil, oregano, and garlic salt. Reduce the heat to low and add the Brie cheese. Stir until the cheese barely melts. Add salt and pepper to taste.

- Divide the pasta between two serving bowls or plates. Pour the sauce over and sprinkle with fresh chopped basil and Kalamata olives.

Try out a new fancy cheese and fruit.

Red and Orange Pasta

4   ounces penne pasta (or other medium-size tube shape)
2   tablespoons oil-packed sun-dried tomatoes, chopped,
    oil reserved
1   large orange
1   teaspoon olive oil
2   cloves garlic, thinly sliced
1   tablespoon brown sugar
1   14-ounce can crushed tomatoes, undrained
1   teaspoon red pepper flakes
    Salt and pepper to taste
1   tablespoon chopped fresh basil
2   ounces Mozzarella cheese, cut into $\frac{1}{2}$-inch cubes

Equipment
Large pot
Medium bowl
Cheese grater or citrus-
    zesting tool
Juicer
Small bowl
Medium saucepan

Servings
2

Preparation Time
15 minutes

Total Time
15 minutes

- In a large pot of boiling salted water cook the penne until tender but still firm to bite. Drain and place in a medium bowl. Add the sun-dried tomatoes with their oil, and toss well to coat. Keep the pasta warm in an oven set on low.

- Meanwhile, with the fine holes of a cheese grater or with a citrus-zesting tool grate about 1 teaspoon of the peel from the orange, being careful not to grate any of the white pith. Cut the orange in half and use a juicer to squeeze all the juice out of it into a small bowl.

- In a medium saucepan heat the olive oil over medium heat. Add the orange zest and garlic. Cook for 3 minutes, stirring occasionally.

- Add $\frac{1}{4}$ cup of the freshly squeezed orange juice, the brown sugar, crushed tomatoes and their juices, and red pepper flakes; increase the heat to high and bring to a boil. Reduce the heat to medium and cook for about 8 minutes. Add salt and pepper to taste.

- Divide the pasta between two serving bowls or plates. Pour the sauce over and sprinkle with basil and Mozzarella cheese. Serve immediately.

Zucchini and Mushroom Marsala

Equipment
Large saucepan
Medium bowl
Medium skillet
Small bowl

Servings
2

Preparation Time
10 minutes

Total Time
10 minutes

6	ounces angel hair pasta
2	teaspoons butter
1	cup green onions, sliced into ½-inch pieces
8	ounces mushrooms, cleaned, trimmed, and sliced
2	small zucchini, rinsed and sliced
¼	cup white wine
⅓	cup Marsala wine
½	teaspoon garlic salt
½	teaspoon Accént or MSG (optional)
1	tablespoon cornstarch
1	teaspoon water

- In a large pot of boiling salted water cook the pasta until tender but still firm to bite. Angel hair cooks fast, so taste it every minute or so until it is done. Drain and place the pasta in a medium bowl. Add 1 teaspoon butter and toss until the butter melts and the pasta is coated. Keep the pasta warm in an oven set on low.

- Meanwhile, in a medium skillet melt the remaining 1 teaspoon butter over medium heat. Add the onions, mushrooms, zucchini slices, and white wine; sauté for 3 to 4 minutes or until the zucchini just starts to lose its crispness.

- Add the Marsala wine, garlic salt, and MSG to the skillet. Sauté for about 3 more minutes.

- In a small bowl whisk the cornstarch with 1 teaspoon water until completely blended. Drizzle into the skillet, stirring constantly. The sauce will thicken immediately, so use only as much as is needed.

- Divide the pasta between two serving bowls or plates. Pour the zucchini sauce over it. Serve immediately.

Zucchini Marinara

Pasta without the pasta—a healthy alternative for people who are watching their weight or limiting their carbohydrate intake. Zucchini has a very mild flavor so it works quite well as a "base" for the flavorful sauce.

2	large fresh zucchini
1	cup of your favorite pasta sauce (try Katy's Garlic Mushroom Red Sauce, p. 117, or Doc's Super-Secret Special Meat Sauce, p. 90)
	Freshly grated Parmesan cheese

- Rinse the zucchini and pat dry. Using the shredder blade of a food processor or the ¼-inch holes of a cheese grater, shred the zucchini.

- Place the shredded zucchini on a double or triple layer of paper towels. Top with more paper towels. Press and squeeze the zucchini until the towels have absorbed most of the moisture. The idea is to get the zucchini pretty dry because it will release its water when you top it with the heated sauce.

- In a small saucepan heat the pasta sauce until hot. Divide the zucchini between two serving bowls or plates. Pour the sauce on top and sprinkle with freshly grated Parmesan cheese.

Equipment
Food processor or cheese grater
Small saucepan

Servings
2

Serving Suggestions
Serve this with thick slices of garlic bread and a tossed salad with vinaigrette dressing.

Preparation Time
10 minutes

Total Time
10 minutes

Bring home take-out occasionally.

Cheesy Onion and Mushroom Enchiladas

This recipe makes enough to give you leftovers for a day or two. The left-overs are very microwaveable, so put two enchiladas in a plastic lunch container and take them to work with you. As a variation, we sometimes add shredded cooked chicken to the mushroom mixture.

3	teaspoons butter
½	cup chopped onion
1	clove garlic, minced
2	15-ounce cans diced tomatoes
2	teaspoons honey
½	teaspoon ground cumin
¼	teaspoon cayenne pepper
3	teaspoons chili powder
1	pound mushrooms, sliced
8	ounces light cream cheese, diced (easiest when cheese is well chilled and firm)
¾	cup sliced green onions
1	cup light sour cream
8	flour tortillas, approximately 9 inches in diameter
½	cup light Pepper Jack cheese, grated

- Preheat the oven to 350°F. Lightly grease a 9 x 13-inch glass baking dish.

- In a large saucepan melt 2 teaspoons butter over medium-high heat. Add the onion and garlic and sauté until tender, about 5 minutes. Stir in the tomatoes with their juices, honey, cumin, cayenne pepper, and 1 teaspoon of the chili powder.

- Bring to a boil; reduce the heat. Simmer, uncovered, for about 30 minutes, stirring occasionally.

- Meanwhile, in a medium saucepan cook the mushrooms and the remaining chili powder in the remaining

*Serve the meal on a single plate and
share the meal. If you both want to lose
weight, use only one set of silverware.*

1 teaspoon butter for about 5 minutes over medium-high heat, until the mushrooms are tender and their liquid evaporates.

- Reduce the heat and add the cream cheese. Stir until melted, and remove from the heat. Add the green onions and ¼ cup of the sour cream and stir until blended.

- Lay one tortilla on a clean counter or cutting board. Spoon about ⅓ cup of the mushroom mixture down the center. Roll up and place, seam side down, in the prepared baking dish. Repeat with the remaining tortillas. Evenly pour the tomato mixture over the enchiladas.

- Cover the pan with aluminum foil and bake for 30 minutes. Uncover, top with the Pepper Jack cheese and remaining sour cream, and bake for an additional 5 minutes, or until the cheese melts and is bubbly.

- Serve hot.

Salads

Club Salad

This is a terrific way to use up holiday turkey leftovers! We like using large pasta plates for salads like this (large dinner-plate size with a shallow bowl indention in the center). You can add any kind of topping or leftover you have on hand—chopped vegetables, leftover roasted potatoes, sun-dried tomatoes, hard-boiled eggs, etc.

2	slices bacon
4	cups shredded lettuce (iceberg, Romaine, leaf, spinach, or any combination)
4	ounces cooked turkey breast or lunchmeat, cubed
2	ounces Swiss cheese, cubed
¼	cup crumbled blue cheese
1	Roma tomato, diced
½	small red onion, sliced
¼	cup honey-roasted pecans
	Croutons
	Honey-mustard or other salad dressing

- Place the bacon slices on a double layer of paper towels. Cover with another double layer of paper towels and place on a plate in the microwave. Microwave for 2 to 3 minutes, or until the bacon is crisp. Let cool, and crumble.

- Divide the lettuce among two dinner plates. Top the salads with the bacon, turkey breast, Swiss cheese, blue cheese, tomato, onion, pecans, and croutons.

- Serve with honey-mustard dressing on the side.

Equipment
Nothing special required.

Servings
2

Serving Suggestions
- Crackers such as saltines or wheat crackers
- Iced tea

Preparation Time
10 minutes

Total Time
10 minutes

Festival Pasta Salad

This salad is infinitely variable. You can use pretty much any chopped vegetables that you like, in any amount that you like. And the recipe doubles or triples very easily to feed a larger group.

Salad:

4	ounces small shell pasta
2	tablespoons olive oil
1	tablespoon garlic, chopped
4	ounces fresh medium shrimp, peeled and deveined
½	yellow bell pepper
½	red bell pepper
½	green bell pepper
¼	cup oil-packed sun-dried tomatoes
4	ounces sliced mushrooms
½	cup whole or sliced green olives
½	cup frozen corn kernels, thawed

Dressing:

2	tablespoons red wine or balsamic vinegar
½	teaspoon Italian seasoning (or use thyme, basil, or oregano)
¼	teaspoon sugar
¼	teaspoon MSG (Accént)
	Dash cayenne pepper
	Dash nutmeg
	Salt to taste

- In a large pot of boiling salted water cook the pasta until tender but still firm to bite. Drain the pasta, transfer it to a serving bowl, and chill it in the refrigerator while you prepare the rest of the ingredients.

- In a small skillet heat 1 tablespoon of oil over medium heat. When hot, add the garlic and stir for 30 seconds. Add the shrimp and stir for 3 to 4 minutes, until the shrimp turn opaque and are cooked all the way through, but not too long or they will become tough. Remove from the heat and set aside.

Keep fresh fruits, like strawberries, on hand for instant desserts.

- Dice the bell peppers. Drain the sun-dried tomatoes on paper towels and chop.

- Add the shrimp, bell peppers, and sun-dried tomatoes to the cooled pasta along with the sliced mushrooms, olives, and corn. Drizzle the remaining 1 tablespoon oil over the pasta salad and toss to coat.

- In small bowl whisk the vinegar with the Italian seasoning, sugar, MSG, cayenne pepper, and nutmeg. Add salt to taste.

- When ready to serve, pour the dressing over the pasta salad and toss to coat. Serve immediately.

Always have whipped cream and chocolate sauce on hand.

Fresh Southwest Chicken Salad

This salad is light and spicy. Packed with protein, it is great by itself or served on top of a bed of salad greens.

2	boneless skinless chicken breasts
1	or 2 large limes
3	tablespoons olive oil
1	clove garlic, minced
½	teaspoon chili powder
8	ounces frozen corn, thawed
1	15-ounce can black beans, rinsed and drained
	Salt and pepper to taste
½	teaspoon ground cumin
1	15-ounce can diced tomatoes, drained
¼	cup sliced onion
¼	cup chopped fresh cilantro
	Lime wedges and cilantro sprigs (garnish)

- Preheat the oven to 350°F. Spray a baking sheet with vegetable oil spray.

- Place chicken on the prepared baking sheet and bake for 20 to 25 minutes, or until the chicken is done. Check for doneness by cutting open at the thickest part and making sure it is white all the way through. When the chicken is cool enough to handle, cut crosswise into ¼-inch slices.

- Meanwhile, with the fine holes of a cheese grater or with a citrus-zesting tool grate about 1 teaspoon of the peel from the lime, being careful not to grate any of the white pith, and set aside. Cut the lime in half and squeeze all the juice out of it into a medium bowl, using a juicer. You will need about 4 tablespoons total, so use the other lime if necessary.

- In a large skillet heat 1 tablespoon olive oil. Add the garlic and cook just until it sizzles. Add the chili powder and cook, stirring constantly, for 30 seconds.

Remove from the heat and add the lime zest, 2 tablespoons of the lime juice, corn, beans, and salt and pepper to taste, and mix well.

- Add the remaining 2 tablespoons olive oil to the remaining 2 tablespoons lime juice, and stir in the cumin, salt, and pepper to taste. Add the sliced chicken to the bowl and toss to coat.

- Add the corn and bean mixture to the chicken and toss gently to mix. Add the drained tomatoes, onions, and cilantro and toss gently again.

- Serve at room temperature, garnished with lime or lemon wedges and cilantro sprigs.

Location, location, location! Nothing is more romantic than being served a meal in a room with big windows overlooking a city skyline, and a thunderstorm brewing in the background.

Rachel's Superior Greek Salad

This is a great main-dish salad. Serve it with any kind of hot fresh bread; pita bread is especially nice. The salad can feed four when used as a side dish.

Equipment
Large bowl
Small bowl

Serving Suggestions
• Hot fresh pita bread and hummus
• A wedge of feta cheese drizzled with vinaigrette

Servings
2 as a main course

Preparation Time
10 minutes

Total Time
10 minutes

4	cups iceberg lettuce, torn into bite-size pieces
1/4	cup feta cheese, crumbled
2	tablespoons oil-packed sun-dried tomatoes, drained and chopped
1/2	cup thinly sliced red or yellow bell pepper
1/4	cup pitted Kalamata olives, cut in half
1/4	cup sliced cucumber
1/4	cup thinly sliced red onion
2	tablespoons freshly squeezed lemon juice
2	teaspoons red wine vinegar
1	clove garlic, minced
1/4	teaspoon sugar
1/2	teaspoon dried oregano
3	tablespoons olive oil
	Salt and pepper to taste

• In a large bowl toss the lettuce with the feta cheese, sun-dried tomatoes, bell peppers, olives, cucumber, and onions.

• In a small bowl combine the lemon juice, vinegar, garlic, sugar, and oregano. Gradually whisk in the olive oil. Season to taste with salt and pepper.

• Pour the dressing over the salad and toss to coat. Season to taste with salt and pepper.

• Serve immediately.

Sesame-Ginger Chicken Salad

This is a great way to use up leftover chicken or shrimp. As is the case with most salads, feel free to vary the types of vegetables or the amounts. Shredding cabbage is very easy with a large chef's knife or using the slicing blade of a food processor.

1	large carrot
2	cups shredded red cabbage
2	cups shredded green cabbage
½	red bell pepper, cut into very thin strips
1	cup sliced grilled chicken (or cooked peeled shrimp)
¼	cup seasoned rice vinegar
2	tablespoons soy sauce
2	tablespoons vegetable oil
1	tablespoon sesame oil
2	tablespoons chopped peeled fresh ginger or ½ teaspoon ground ginger
1	tablespoon sugar
	Salt and pepper to taste
½	cup dry-roasted salted peanuts
¼	cup thinly sliced green onion
¼	cup chopped cilantro
	Sesame seeds as garnish

Equipment
Food processor or cheese grater
Large bowl
Small bowl

Servings
2 as a main course

Preparation Time
10 minutes

Total Time
10 minutes

- Peel the carrot and shred it with a food processor or the large holes of a cheese grater. In a large bowl combine the carrot with the red and green cabbage, bell pepper, and chicken or shrimp.

- In a small bowl whisk the vinegar with the soy sauce, vegetable oil, sesame oil, ginger, sugar, and salt and pepper to taste. Pour the dressing over the salad, and toss to coat.

- Divide the salad between two serving plates. Top with peanuts, green onions, and cilantro, and sprinkle with sesame seeds.

Classic Potato Salad

Equipment
Large saucepan
Two medium bowls

Servings
4

Serving Suggestions
Some people like to garnish potato salad with slices of hard-boiled egg. We like to use a sprinkle of paprika for color. You can make a great picnic meal by serving this with Flattened Oven-Fried Chicken (p. 91) or Picnic Chicken with Sesame-Citrus Sauce (p. 96).

Preparation Time
10 minutes

Total Time
50 minutes (including chill time)

3   large russet or Idaho baking potatoes, peeled and cut into ½-inch chunks
¼   cup mayonnaise
¼   cup yellow mustard
¼   cup finely minced yellow onion
¼   cup finely minced red or green bell pepper
¼   cup finely minced celery
¼   cup finely minced sweet pickles
   Salt and pepper to taste

• Bring a large saucepan of water to a boil over high heat. Add the potato chunks and boil until tender, about 10 minutes. Drain the potatoes and place them in a medium bowl.

• In another medium bowl mix together the mayonnaise and mustard. Add about half of the potato chunks to the mayonnaise mixture, and mash together with a fork until the mixture is fairly smooth and creamy. Add salt and pepper to taste.

• Add the onion, bell pepper, celery, and pickles to the bowl with the potato chunks. Toss to mix. Add the creamy potato mixture and stir gently until well blended. Chill the potato salad in the refrigerator for at least 30 minutes.

Fast Fresh Fruit Salad

Like most salads, this one can contain any ingredients you like in any amount; in fact, it's a great way to use up your excess fruit before it goes bad. The only constant we recommend is pineapple, because its acidity will prevent the other fruits from browning too quickly from exposure to air. Rinse and pat dry all fresh fruits before using.

½	cup canned pineapple chunks or tidbits, drained
1	tablespoon honey
¼	teaspoon cinnamon (optional)
2	teaspoons lemon juice
½	cup red or green grapes
½	cup strawberries, destemmed and cut in half
1	red or green apple
1	D'anjou or Bartlett pear

- In a medium bowl, mix the pineapple chunks with the honey, cinnamon (if using), and lemon juice. Stir in the grapes and strawberries.

- Peel the apple and pear, if desired. Cut into ½-inch chunks. Add to the pineapple mixture and toss to blend.

Equipment
Medium bowl

Servings
2 to 4

Preparation Time
5 minutes

Total Time
5 minutes

Keep several bottles of wine handy, both white and red.

Super-Fast Salad

Equipment
Nothing special required.

Servings
2

Preparation Time
5 minutes

Total Time
5 minutes

This Austrian recipe produces a simple and colorful salad. If you plan to store the salad, don't cut the lettuce with a metal knife as it will turn brown faster. You can use any salad greens of your choice, but avoid iceberg for this recipe.

1	small head Romaine or other favorite lettuce
2	Roma tomatoes
	Vinaigrette or other salad dressing

- Rinse the lettuce and pat dry, or use a salad spinner. Tear into bite-size pieces.

- Rinse each tomato and cut into 4 to 8 bite-size wedges.

- Combine the lettuce and tomato wedges in a serving bowl. Serve with vinaigrette or your favorite dressing.

Leave a funny or romantic note where your partner will find it.

Thai-Style Pork Salad

If you don't have a meat mallet, you can substitute a can from your pantry, a rolling pin, or even the bottom of a heavy glass.

3 cups shredded green cabbage
¼ cup chopped cilantro
8 large mint leaves, chopped
2 4-ounce boneless pork cutlets (½-inch thick)
1 tablespoon oil
Salt and pepper to taste
2 tablespoons sliced onion
2 tablespoons dry-roasted salted peanuts
Dash cayenne pepper
5 tablespoons lime juice
1 teaspoon sugar

Equipment
Large bowl
Meat mallet
Skillet

Servings
2 as a main course

Preparation Time
20 minutes

Total Time
20 minutes

- In a large bowl toss the cabbage, cilantro, and mint.

- Trim any visible fat from the pork cutlets. Place the cutlets in a plastic zipper bag or between two sheets of plastic wrap and pound with a meat mallet until ¼-inch thick.

- In a skillet heat the oil over medium-high heat. When hot, place the flattened pork cutlets in the skillet and sprinkle with salt and pepper to taste. Let cook for 3 to 4 minutes, then turn over. Cook for another 3 to 4 minutes, or until nicely browned and cooked through.

- Remove the cutlets from the skillet, cool slightly, and slice into ¼-inch strips.

- Place the pork back in the same skillet over medium-high heat, and add the onion, peanuts, and cayenne pepper. Add a little more oil if necessary. Cook and stir for 2 minutes, and remove from the heat. Add the lime juice and sugar. Add salt and pepper to taste.

- Spoon the pork mixture over the cabbage; toss to coat. Serve immediately.

Vegetarian Taco Salad

Equipment
Small bowl
Medium saucepan

Servings
2

Preparation Time
5 minutes

Total Time
10 minutes

You can add some cooked crumbled ground beef to the beans if you want some extra protein in your dinner.

1	15-ounce can black beans, drained and rinsed
4	tablespoons water or chicken broth
1	tablespoon taco seasoning mix (or use garlic salt, cumin powder, and chili powder)
4	cups loosely packed shredded iceberg or Romaine lettuce
½	cup grated Cheddar cheese
1	4-ounce can chopped black olives, drained
2	stalks green onion, thinly sliced
1	Roma tomato, chopped
2	tablespoons sour cream
	Salsa to taste (try Katy's Hot Salsa, p. 157)
	Tortilla chips

- Put about ½ cup of the black beans in a small bowl and mash with a fork. Add 2 tablespoons of the water or chicken broth and mash again until fairly smooth.

- In a medium saucepan combine the mashed beans with the remaining black beans, the remaining 2 tablespoons water or chicken broth, and the taco seasoning mix over medium heat. Cook until the beans are warm, about 5 minutes.

- Spread the lettuce on serving plates. Top with half of the warm black beans, grated Cheddar, black olives, green onion, tomato, sour cream, and salsa.

- Arrange the tortilla chips around the sides of the plates, and serve the salads with extra salsa.

Dressings

Blue Cheese Vinaigrette

2	tablespoons olive oil
2	cloves garlic, minced
1	tablespoon finely minced onion
¾	cup crumbled blue cheese (about 3 ounces)
⅓	cup white wine vinegar
2	teaspoons sugar
½	teaspoon Tabasco sauce
½	teaspoon salt
¼	teaspoon pepper

Equipment
Small saucepan
Blender

Servings
8 (1 cup)

Preparation Time
10 minutes

Total Time
10 minutes

- In a small saucepan heat 1 tablespoon of the oil over medium heat. Add the garlic and onion, and sauté until golden, about 2 minutes.

- Spoon the garlic-onion mixture and its oil into the blender. Add the remaining 1 tablespoon of oil, the blue cheese, vinegar, sugar, Tabasco sauce, salt, and pepper. Blend until fairly smooth, with just a few chunks of blue cheese remaining.

- Pour the dressing into a bottle or cruet, and shake well to blend before serving.

Red French Dressing

This is not the nuclear orange stuff you see in bottles at the supermarket! Nor is it authentic "French Dressing," which is simply mustard, oil, vinegar, salt, and pepper (see recipe on p. 147).

(see recipe on p. 147)

Equipment
Jar with tight-fitting lid
or blender

Servings
20 (1¼ cups)

Preparation Time
5 minutes

Total Time
5 minutes

⅓ cup sugar

2 teaspoons salt

1 tablespoon paprika

1 teaspoon black pepper

¼ cup vegetable oil

3 tablespoons yellow mustard

¾ cup white or cider vinegar

¼ cup ketchup

1 clove garlic, halved

• In a jar with a tight-fitting lid or in a blender mix the sugar, salt, paprika, and pepper.

• Add the oil to the dry ingredients and blend, or shake the jar vigorously until well mixed.

• Add the mustard, vinegar, and ketchup. Blend or shake the jar until the mixture is smooth and the oil does not separate.

• Pour the dressing into a bottle or cruet with the garlic halves (or simply leave it in the shaker jar). You may use the dressing immediately, or refrigerate it overnight to let the flavors blend.

Kathryn's Authentic French Dressing

Kathryn lived in France for a year and brought this simple recipe back with her. She would prepare it in a little flowered teacup in our college apartment.

2 tablespoons Dijon mustard
1 tablespoon red or white wine vinegar
2 tablespoons olive oil
Salt and pepper to taste

- In a small bowl slowly whisk the vinegar into the mustard. Whisk in the olive oil until the mixture is smooth and the oil does not separate. Add the salt and pepper to taste, and stir to blend well.

- Pour the dressing into a bottle or cruet, and shake well to blend before serving.

Note
This recipe makes enough for two dinner-size salads or four side salad servings. Experiment with different kinds of mustard and vinegar for a variety of flavors.

Equipment
Small bowl

Servings
2

Preparation Time
5 minutes

Total Time
5 minutes

To make any meal just a little more special, serve dinner rolls on the side, in a basket lined with a colorful napkin or cloth.

Lemon Vinaigrette

A very light-tasting lemony dressing, which is great not only on salads but as a dip for veggies or a sauce for pasta.

¼ cup lemon juice

2 cloves garlic, minced

½ cup olive oil

½ cup freshly grated Parmesan cheese

1 teaspoon dried oregano leaves

1 teaspoon sugar

Salt and pepper to taste

- In a blender mix the lemon juice and garlic until the garlic is chopped finely.

- Pour in the olive oil and blend until the mixture is smooth and the oil does not separate.

- Add the Parmesan cheese, oregano, and sugar, and blend until the dressing is thick. Add salt and pepper to taste.

- Pour the dressing into a bottle or cruet, and shake well to blend before serving.

Equipment
Blender

Servings
8 (1 cup)

Serving Suggestions
- Salad of mixed field greens
- Try it over chilled pasta with chopped fresh vegetables
- Great with citrusy white wines such as Riesling

Preparation Time
5 minutes

Total Time
5 minutes

Lighter Lemon Vinaigrette

¼ cup lemon juice

1 tablespoon white vinegar

1 clove garlic, minced

2 tablespoons olive oil

1 teaspoon dried oregano leaves

¼ teaspoon sugar

   Salt and pepper to taste

- In a small bowl mix the lemon juice, vinegar, and garlic.

- Add the oil and whisk thoroughly until the mixture is smooth and the oil does not separate. Add the oregano, sugar, and salt and pepper to taste.

- Pour the dressing into a bottle or cruet, and shake well to blend before serving.

Equipment
Small bowl

Servings
4 (½ cup)

Preparation Time
5 minutes

Total Time
5 minutes

Go to the state or county fair, eat a corny dog or funnel cake, and act silly all evening.

Poppy Seed Dressing

Be careful of the fumes when heating vinegar. While not harmful, they can be overpowering. Open a window or use the stove fan.

½   cup cider or white vinegar

½   cup sugar

⅓   cup chopped onion

½   teaspoon dry mustard

½   teaspoon salt

½   cup vegetable oil

2   teaspoons poppy seeds

Equipment
Medium saucepan
Blender
Cheesecloth
Small bowl

Servings
12 (1 cup)

Serving Suggestions
Spinach salad with grilled chicken breast and mandarin orange sections or sliced strawberries

Preparation Time
15 minutes

Total Time
15 minutes

- In a medium saucepan heat the vinegar and sugar together over medium heat until the sugar dissolves, about 5 minutes, stirring constantly. Let the syrup cool in the refrigerator until needed.

- In a blender purée the chopped onion. Scrape the onion purée out into a piece of cheesecloth or several layers of strong paper towels. Squeeze the cheesecloth over a small bowl to catch the onion juice. Measure out 1 tablespoon and add it to the vinegar syrup. Discard the onion purée and leftover juice.

- Add the dry mustard and salt to the vinegar syrup. Pour the mixture into the clean blender jar. With the motor running, add the oil slowly until the mixture is smooth and the oil does not separate. Stir in the poppy seeds.

- Pour the dressing into a bottle or cruet, and refrigerate until ready to serve. Bring to room temperature before serving.

- Note: Do not use olive oil for this dressing. The flavor is too strong. A lighter version of this dressing can be made by using only ¼ cup oil.

Salsa Ranch Dressing

This is a perfect accompaniment to any kind of salad, especially a taco or fajita salad. It also works great as a dip for vegetables.

½ cup buttermilk

1 cup mayonnaise (regular or light)

1 package Hidden Valley Ranch dressing mix (buttermilk recipe)

1 cup Katy's Hot Salsa, p. 157, or other favorite salsa

- In a medium bowl blend together the buttermilk, mayonnaise, and Ranch dressing with a whisk or a fork until smooth. Stir in the salsa.

- Use immediately, or let the dressing chill for several hours to thicken and let the flavors blend.

Equipment
Medium bowl

Servings
18 (2¼ cups)

Preparation Time
5 minutes

Total Time
5 minutes

Thousand Island Dressing

½ cup mayonnaise

½ cup ketchup

¼ cup pickle relish or chopped sweet pickles

Cayenne pepper and salt to taste

Equipment
Small bowl

Servings
10 (1¼ cups)

Preparation Time
5 minutes

Total Time
5 minutes

- In a small bowl stir together the mayonnaise, ketchup, relish or pickles, cayenne pepper, and salt, using a whisk or a fork. Pour the dressing into a bottle or cruet.

- Use immediately, or let the dressing chill for several hours to let the flavors blend.

Eating somewhere unusual—a balcony, an apartment rooftop, or in a garden—can make a meal more exciting and more romantic.

Sauces

Creamy Teriyaki Sauce

This is an unusual creamy variation on the standard teriyaki sauce. It is not suited for use as a marinade; it's more like a dip or dressing.

2	tablespoons brown sugar
1	cup sour cream
½	teaspoon powdered ginger or 1 teaspoon fresh minced ginger
2	cloves garlic, minced
2	teaspoons Sherry cooking wine
3	tablespoons soy sauce

- In a small bowl whisk the brown sugar into the sour cream. Add the ginger and garlic, and whisk until blended.

- Slowly add the Sherry and soy sauce, blending constantly with whisk until incorporated.

Equipment
Small bowl

Serving Suggestions
This sauce goes nicely with any Asian-influenced salad, such as a cabbage salad with chicken. It also makes an unusual dipping sauce for vegetable sticks.

Servings
4

Preparation Time
5 minutes

Total Time
5 minutes

Meuniere Sauce

This is a wonderful Cajun/Creole sauce commonly served atop blackened meat dishes. It is tangy, spicy, and very buttery. Any extra will keep for a while in the refrigerator, and can be used on any number of dishes. It can serve as a reasonable substitute for Hollandaise Sauce.

½	cup (1 stick) butter
3	tablespoons lemon juice
2	tablespoons minced green onions
1	tablespoon minced parsley
¼	teaspoon pepper
¼	teaspoon salt
3	tablespoons Worcestershire sauce
½	teaspoon sugar
	Dash Tabasco sauce

- In a small saucepan melt the butter over medium-high heat. When melted, add the lemon juice, green onions, parsley, pepper, salt, Worcestershire sauce, sugar, and Tabasco sauce. Reduce the heat to medium-low, and simmer for 5 minutes.

- Pour the sauce into a serving dish, and serve with blackened fish or chicken.

Equipment
Small saucepan

Serving Suggestions
- Blackened fish or chicken
- Rice
- Mixed steamed vegetables

Servings
8

Preparation Time
10 minutes

Total Time
10 minutes

Teriyaki Sauce

Teriyaki can be used as a marinade for meats or vegetables, or as a dipping sauce for grilled meats, vegetables, egg rolls, or wontons. Try it drizzled over fried rice as a nice substitute for soy sauce.

⅓	cup soy sauce
2	tablespoons brown sugar
2	tablespoons Sherry cooking wine
½	teaspoon powdered ginger or 1 teaspoon fresh minced ginger
2	cloves garlic, minced
	Salt and pepper to taste

- In a small bowl combine the soy sauce with the brown sugar. Whisk until blended and the sugar is dissolved.

- Add the Sherry, ginger, garlic, and salt and pepper to taste. Stir until blended.

- Store, covered, in the refrigerator until needed.

Put your favorite music on the stereo, softly, during the meal.

Equipment
Small bowl

Servings
2

Serving Suggestions
Great as a marinade or dipping sauce for chicken or pork.

Preparation Time
5 minutes

Total Time
5 minutes

Tomato Chutney

Chutney is quite popular served with meat—try it with Quick Sliced Pork Sandwiches, p. 98. It is also tasty on grilled vegetables.

1	28-ounce can diced tomatoes with juices
¼	cup sugar
⅓	cup apple cider vinegar
1	cinnamon stick, broken in half
1½	teaspoons ground cardamom
2	teaspoons cumin seeds
1	bay leaf
3	tablespoons chopped peeled ginger
	Salt and pepper to taste

Equipment
Strainer
Large saucepan

Servings
8

Preparation Time
5 minutes

Total Time
30 minutes

- Set a strainer over a large saucepan on high heat. Pour the tomatoes into the strainer and drain the juices into the pan. Reserve the tomatoes for later.

- Add the sugar, vinegar, cinnamon, cardamom, cumin, bay leaf, and ginger to the tomato juices and boil until reduced by half, about 10 minutes.

- Add the tomatoes to the pan and simmer over medium heat until the chutney thickens, about 12 minutes. Remove from the heat. Season to taste with salt and pepper.

- Serve chilled or at room temperature.

Eat outside on nice evenings.

Katy's Hot Salsa

This salsa is very spicy. To make a milder version, use fewer jalapeño peppers, or use mild or medium Rotel-brand tomatoes. Arushi and Shyamal can polish off a large jar of this in under a week.

1	28-ounce can crushed tomatoes or tomato purée
1	14-ounce can diced tomatoes
1	10-ounce can regular or extra-hot Rotel-brand diced tomatoes with chilies
1	6-ounce can tomato paste
2	to 3 large fresh jalapeño peppers
6	tablespoons white or cider vinegar
1	medium onion, finely chopped
1	cup chopped cilantro leaves, loosely packed
1	tablespoon ground cumin
2	teaspoons chili powder
2	teaspoons garlic salt
1	teaspoon sugar
1	teaspoon MSG or Accént (optional)
½	teaspoon ground oregano

Note
Do not store homemade jars of salsa in the pantry—doing so requires a jar sterilization and boiling-water canning process to kill bacteria and make it safe to store on the shelf.

Equipment
Large pot
Four pint-size canning jars

Servings
About 7 cups

Preparation Time
15 minutes

Total Time
45 minutes

- In a large pot combine the crushed tomatoes, diced tomatoes, Rotel tomatoes, and tomato paste over medium heat.

- Remove the seeds and ribs from the jalapeño peppers if you wish (leaving them in makes a much hotter salsa). Finely chop the jalapeños and add them to the pot along with the vinegar, onion, and cilantro leaves.

- Let the salsa come to a simmer, and cook for 10 minutes, stirring occasionally. Add the cumin, chili powder, garlic salt, sugar, MSG or Accént (if using), and oregano. Mix thoroughly. Cover and simmer for an additional 15 to 20 minutes, stirring occasionally.

- Remove from the heat. Very carefully ladle the hot salsa into pint-size canning jars and tightly screw on the lids. Store in the refrigerator for up to three months.

Side Dishes

Baked French Fries

1 large Idaho baking potato
2 tablespoons olive oil
  Salt, pepper, and chili powder to taste

- Preheat the oven to 425°F.

- Scrub the potato under cool running water and pat dry. Peel with a vegetable peeler, and cut out any visible brown spots with a small paring knife.

- Cut the potato lengthwise into ¼-inch thick slices. Cut each slice into long "planks" about ¾-inch wide. Rinse in a colander or strainer under cool running water. The idea is to rinse away the surface starch, which will help keep the potatoes from sticking to the baking sheet. Drain the potatoes and pat dry with paper towels.

- Place the potato planks into a large zip-top plastic bag and drizzle with 1 tablespoon of the olive oil. Shake the bag to coat thoroughly.

- Drizzle the remaining 1 tablespoon olive oil on the baking sheet and spread it around. Arrange the potatoes in a single layer on the baking sheet, and sprinkle with salt, pepper, and chili powder to taste.

- Bake for 20 to 25 minutes or until crispy, turning fries once during cooking.

Equipment
Vegetable peeler
Colander or strainer
Baking sheet

Servings
2

Serving Suggestions
Great with any type of sandwich or grilled chicken.

Preparation Time
10 minutes

Total Time
30 minutes

Baked Onion Rings

1   medium yellow onion
2   tablespoons olive oil
1½ cups corn flakes, or ¾ cup bread crumbs,
     or 16 Saltine crackers
½   teaspoon garlic salt
¼   teaspoon pepper
½   teaspoon chili powder
1   tablespoon flour

Equipment
Baking sheet

Servings
2

Serving Suggestions
Great with any type of
sandwich or grilled chicken.

Preparation Time
10 minutes

Total Time
30 minutes

• Preheat the oven to 425°F.

• Cut a thin slice off of the root end and top of onion.
  Remove the papery skin and slice the onion horizontally into ½-inch thick rings. Separate the rings and place
  into a large zip-top plastic bag. Drizzle with 1 tablespoon of the olive oil. Shake the bag to coat thoroughly.

• In another large zip-top plastic bag, crush the corn
  flakes, breadcrumbs, or saltines until they are very fine.
  (You can also use a food processor for this.) Add the
  garlic salt, pepper, chili powder, and flour, and shake to
  mix thoroughly.

• Pour the crumb mixture into the plastic bag with the
  onions, and shake to coat thoroughly.

• Drizzle the remaining 1 tablespoon olive oil on the baking sheet and spread it around. Arrange the onion rings
  in a single layer on the baking sheet.

• Bake for 20 to 25 minutes or until crispy, turning once
  during cooking.

Burgundy Mushrooms

2	teaspoons olive oil
1	cup sliced yellow onion
1	clove garlic, minced
8	ounces small mushrooms, cleaned and trimmed
½	cup burgundy or other favorite red wine
1	teaspoon chicken bouillon granules (or 1 cube)

Salt and pepper to taste

- In a medium saucepan heat the olive oil over medium heat. Add the onion and garlic and cook, stirring, for about 5 minutes or until the onion is golden and translucent.

- If the mushrooms are large, cut them in half or fourths. Add the mushrooms to the saucepan and cook, stirring, for an additional 5 minutes.

- Add the wine, chicken bouillon, and pepper to taste. Increase the heat and bring the mixture to a boil. Reduce the heat to medium and simmer for 5 minutes.

- Add the salt and pepper to taste. Serve hot.

The person who cooks gets the night off from doing dishes.

Equipment
Medium saucepan

Servings
2 to 4

Serving Suggestions
Great with red meat such as a steak, or even a pork cutlet.

Preparation Time
10 minutes

Total Time
20 minutes

Cilantro Rice

Equipment
Medium saucepan

Servings
2

Preparation Time
10 minutes

Total Time
30 minutes

2   teaspoons olive oil
½   cup chopped yellow onion
1   small Roma tomato, diced
½   cup finely minced cilantro
1   clove garlic, minced
1   cup chicken or vegetable broth
½   cup rice
     Salt and pepper to taste

- In a medium saucepan heat the olive oil over medium-high heat. Sauté the onion and tomato for about 3 minutes, until the onion is beginning to soften.

- Add the cilantro, garlic, chicken broth, and rice. Bring to a boil. Reduce the heat to medium-low, cover the pan, and cook without stirring for about 20 minutes, or until the rice is tender and the liquid is absorbed. Season with salt and pepper to taste.

Corn with Lemon Butter

This is an easy and delicious way to dress up a classic side dish.

1	tablespoon butter
8	ounces frozen corn, thawed and drained
½	teaspoon ground thyme
½	teaspoon sugar
2	teaspoons fresh lemon juice
	Salt and pepper to taste
	Ground thyme (garnish)
	Snipped fresh chives (garnish)

Equipment
Large saucepan

Servings
2

Preparation Time
10 minutes

Total Time
10 minutes

- In a large saucepan melt the butter over medium-high heat. Add the corn and cook for several minutes, until heated through.

- Stir in the thyme, sugar, and lemon juice, and cook another 5 minutes, stirring occasionally.

- Season the corn to taste with salt and pepper. Spoon into a serving bowl, and top with a sprinkling of thyme and chives.

*Get out the camera and commemorate
the special occasion of tonight's dinner!*

Doc's Sautéed Asparagus

Most asparagus is served steamed, but Doc has a really unique way of preparing it. It stays quite crisp and has a wonderful garlic flavor.

Equipment	
Large skillet	

Servings
2

Preparation Time
15 minutes

Total Time
15 minutes

½   pound fresh thin asparagus (about ¼-inch diameter stalks)

2   teaspoons butter

1   teaspoon minced garlic

    Salt and pepper to taste

    Grated fresh Parmesan cheese to taste

- Rinse the asparagus and trim each stalk by holding the tip and the end and bending until it breaks naturally. Discard the bottom ends. Drain the stalks on paper towels and pat dry.

- In a large skillet melt the butter over medium-high heat. Add the asparagus and sauté for about 5 minutes.

- Turn the heat to medium-low. Add the garlic and cook for an additional 2 to 3 minutes, until the asparagus stalks are crisp-tender and bright green. Don't let the asparagus overcook or it will turn dull in color and become mushy. Season to taste with salt and pepper.

- Remove from the pan to a serving platter. Sprinkle with Parmesan cheese and serve.

Save dessert for after romantic interludes.

Greek Rice Florentine

Be sure to use fresh spinach leaves for this. Frozen spinach will turn the whole thing into mush. Texture is as important as taste in this recipe.

1	tablespoon olive oil
¾	cup chopped onion
2	large cloves garlic, minced
¾	cup long-grain white rice
⅓	cup white wine
1	tablespoon lemon juice
1	cup chicken broth
8	ounces fresh spinach leaves (not frozen)
2	tablespoons oil-packed sun-dried tomatoes
1	small Roma tomato, chopped
½	cup cubed feta cheese, (about 2 ounces)
2	tablespoons chopped Kalamata olives
	Salt and pepper to taste

- In a large pot heat the olive oil over medium-high heat. Add the onion and garlic and sauté until the onion is translucent and tender, about 5 minutes.

- Add the rice and stir until translucent, about 2 minutes. Add the wine, lemon juice, and chicken broth, and bring to a boil. Reduce the heat to low so that the mixture is barely simmering. Cover and cook for about 15 minutes, or until the rice is almost tender.

- Meanwhile, rinse, pat dry, and coarsely chop the spinach leaves. Add to the rice mixture. Cover and cook until the rice and spinach are tender and all liquid is absorbed, about 7 minutes longer. Remove from heat.

- Drain the oil from the sun-dried tomatoes on paper towels. Pat dry and chop. Carefully and gently fold into the rice mixture along with the chopped Roma tomato, feta cheese, and olives. Do not overmix or the rice will turn out mushy. Season with salt and pepper and serve.

Equipment
Large pot

Servings
2 to 3

Serving Suggestions
Simple grilled fish or chicken breast

Preparation Time
15 minutes

Total Time
35 minutes

Equipment
Large pot
Small bowl

Servings
2

Serving Suggestions
• Simple grilled fish or chicken breast
• Spicy Potato Gratin (p. 169)

Preparation Time
10 minutes

Total Time
10 minutes

Sautéed Green Beans

1½ cups fresh green beans, trimmed
1   clove garlic, minced
1   teaspoon olive oil
½   teaspoon paprika
¼   teaspoon ground cumin
3   tablespoons fresh lemon juice
    Salt and pepper to taste

• Bring a large pot of water to a boil over high heat. Add the green beans and cook for 2 minutes. Drain, and transfer the beans to a serving bowl.

• In a small bowl whisk together the garlic, olive oil, paprika, cumin, and lemon juice. Season to taste with salt and pepper. Pour over the green beans and toss to coat.

• Serve hot.

Drink a cocktail or a glass of wine before dinner while listening to old blues and jazz tunes.

Grilled Corn on the Cob

Corn cooked this way tastes very fresh and sweet, which contrasts wonderfully with the salt and spices.

2   ears corn on the cob
2   teaspoons butter
    Salt
    Chili powder

- Heat a barbecue grill to medium-hot.

- Remove the husks and silks from the corn, if any.

- Tear two sheets of aluminum foil about 12 inches square. Lay an ear of corn on each sheet. Spread one teaspoon of butter on each ear of corn, covering all sides, and sprinkle with salt and chili powder. Roll the corn up in the foil, pinching the ends to seal.

- Cook the corn on the grill for about 20 minutes, turning several times during cooking.

- Remove from the grill and carefully unwrap the corn and transfer to a serving plate. Corn kernels can also be sliced off the cob and transferred to a bowl for serving.

Equipment
Barbecue grill

Servings
2

Preparation Time
5 minutes

Total Time
25 minutes

Lemon Olive Rice

This rice dish is healthy, cooks quickly, and has a wonderful light Mediterranean flavor.

Equipment
Cheese grater or citrus-zesting tool
Medium saucepan

Servings
2 to 4

Serving Suggestions
• Spicy marinated grilled chicken
• Pineapple chunks or rings

Preparation Time
5 minutes

Total Time
25 minutes

1	lemon
1	cup long-grain white rice
2	cups water
¼	cup pitted Kalamata olives, coarsely chopped
2	tablespoons chopped green onions or chives
	Lemon pepper to taste

• Rinse the lemon and pat dry. With the fine holes of a cheese grater or with a citrus-zesting tool, grate about 1 teaspoon of the peel from the lemon, being careful not to grate any of the white pith. Cut the lemon into quarters and set aside.

• In a medium saucepan combine the lemon zest, rice, and water. Bring to a boil over high heat. Reduce the heat to medium-low, cover the pot, and let the rice simmer until it is cooked through and all the water is absorbed, about 15 to 20 minutes. Don't stir the rice or lift the lid while it is cooking.

• Remove the pan from the heat and stir in the chopped olives and green onions. Sprinkle generously with lemon pepper to taste. Serve with lemon quarters.

Spicy Potato Gratin

This potato gratin is lower in calories than the traditional version, but it doesn't taste like it. You could add any number of "extras" to the gratin—try sun-dried tomatoes, spinach, jalapeño or red bell peppers, or onions.

1   tablespoon butter

1   clove garlic, minced

1   teaspoon Tabasco sauce (or to taste)

1   pound small red potatoes

½   teaspoon salt

¼   teaspoon ground black pepper

½   cup shredded cheese, loosely packed (Cheddar, Swiss, Parmesan, Gruyere, or any combination of your favorite cheeses)

½   cup low-fat milk

- Preheat the oven to 425°F. Spray an 8-inch square or round glass baking dish with vegetable oil spray.

- In a small saucepan heat the butter until melted. Add the garlic and Tabasco sauce and stir to mix.

- Rinse the potatoes (do not peel) and slice into ⅛-inch slices in a food processor or with a knife.

- Layer half of the potatoes in the baking dish. Drizzle with half the garlic butter, and sprinkle with half the salt, pepper, and grated cheese. Add another layer of potatoes, garlic butter, salt, pepper, and cheese.

- In another small saucepan heat the milk over medium-low heat just until it boils. Immediately remove from the heat and pour over the potatoes.

- Bake for 40 minutes, or until the cheese on top is golden-brown and the gratin is bubbly.

Equipment
8-inch square or round glass baking dish
Two small saucepans
Food processor or knife

Servings
4

Serving Suggestions
We love this served with a tossed green salad and a bowl of Classic Tomato Soup (p. 179).

Preparation Time
20 minutes

Total Time
1 hour

Grilled Vegetables

You can use any or all of these vegetables, or substitute your own favorites. Cubed potatoes (pre-boiled for about 10 minutes) work very well, as does firm tofu in chunks. Remember that softer vegetables will be done in about 5 minutes, and firmer ones take 10 to 15 minutes.

1   cup fresh mushrooms, sliced in half if large
½   cup onions, sliced ½-inch thick
1   small red bell pepper, cut into chunks
1   small zucchini, sliced ¼-inch thick
½   cup cherry tomatoes
1   tablespoon olive oil
One of the following marinades:
Balsamic Rosemary Marinade:
  3   tablespoons balsamic vinegar
  1   teaspoon dried rosemary
  ½   teaspoon Tabasco sauce
       Salt and pepper to taste
Teriyaki Marinade:
  1   teaspoon sesame oil
  2   tablespoons white wine vinegar
  1   tablespoon Sherry cooking wine
  1   tablespoon soy sauce
  2   teaspoons minced fresh ginger
  1   teaspoon brown sugar, packed
  ½   teaspoon Tabasco sauce
  1   clove garlic, minced
       Salt and pepper to taste
Citrus Marinade:
  3   tablespoons freshly squeezed lemon juice
  1   teaspoon lemon zest
  2   teaspoons orange zest
  1   teaspoon white wine vinegar
       Salt and pepper to taste

- Place the vegetables into a large plastic zipper bag. Drizzle the olive oil over them and shake to coat.

- In a small bowl combine the ingredients for whichever marinade you prefer. Season with salt and pepper to taste.

- Pour the marinade over the vegetables and shake the bag to coat. Let sit for 20 minutes, turning the bag occasionally.

- Heat the barbecue grill to medium-hot.

- Place the vegetables in a grill wok or basket and put on the barbecue, about 4 to 6 inches above the heat. (Alternatively, you can thread the veggies onto metal skewers [tomatoes and mushrooms on separate skewers from the zucchini, peppers, and onions] and place the skewers on the grill.)

- Grill the tomatoes and mushrooms for about 5 minutes, stirring frequently, before removing from the heat with a large spoon. Cook the zucchini, peppers, and onions 5 to 10 minutes longer, stirring frequently to grill all sides. Everything should be lightly browned and still crisp-tender.

- Season with salt and pepper to taste before serving.

Make up a silly story about how you might have first met.

Notes

A nonstick grill wok is a very handy item to have for grilling small items like shrimp or vegetables. The kind we use is square, with sloping sides, and covered in $1/4$-inch holes.

You can also make this recipe as shish kabobs, but skewered vegetables often refuse to turn when you turn the skewer. This happens because as they cook, they shrink a little—and the hole made by the skewer enlarges. This is remedied somewhat if you have slightly flattened skewers instead of round ones. Also, you can buy "skewer baskets" for the grill—long narrow baskets with tops that close down to secure the vegetables or meat for easy turning.

171

Spicy Corn with Lime Cream Sauce

Equipment
Small bowl
Large skillet

Servings
2

Serving Suggestions
• Magical Southwestern Black Beans, p. 118
• Chips and salsa
• Mexican beer, such as Corona

Preparation Time
10 minutes

Total Time
25 minutes

¼   cup sour cream
¼   teaspoon chili powder
¼   teaspoon ground cumin
½   teaspoon Tabasco sauce, or to taste
3   tablespoons cilantro, chopped
1   tablespoon lime juice
    Salt and pepper to taste
2   teaspoons oil
1½ cups frozen corn, thawed
½   jalapeño pepper, seeded and diced
¼   cup minced red onion
1   small Roma tomato, chopped

- In a small bowl combine the sour cream with the chili powder, cumin, Tabasco sauce, and 1 tablespoon of the chopped cilantro. Slowly whisk the lime juice into the sour cream, just a little at a time. Season to taste with salt and pepper. Set aside.

- In a large skillet heat the oil over high heat. Add the corn and sauté for about 2 minutes. Add the jalapeño pepper, onion, and tomato, and cook for another 2 minutes. Season to taste with salt and pepper.

- Transfer the corn mixture to a serving bowl and let it cool in the refrigerator for about 15 minutes. When cooled, pour the lime cream sauce over the corn and toss to coat. Sprinkle the remaining 2 tablespoons chopped cilantro over salad. Serve chilled or at room temperature.

Mom's Baked Beans

These beans are even better the next day! Dad adds jalapeño peppers to his version, but we think the beans are terrific without them.

¼	pound lean bacon
4	medium yellow onions, chopped
½	cup brown sugar, packed
2	tablespoons molasses
¼ to ½	teaspoon cayenne pepper
1	teaspoon liquid smoke (optional)
1	28-ounce can "pork & beans," undrained

- Chop the bacon into ½-inch pieces (this is easier to do if the bacon is somewhat frozen).

- In a large pot cook the bacon over medium-high heat, stirring frequently, for about 5 minutes.

- Add the chopped onions and continue cooking until the onions are translucent and the bacon has started to get crisp and browned.

- Add the brown sugar, molasses, cayenne pepper, liquid smoke, and beans with their liquid to the pot. Bring to a boil, then reduce the heat to low.

- Simmer, stirring occasionally, for 30 minutes to 2 hours, depending on how much time you have. The longer you cook the beans, the better the flavor.

- Serve hot or cold.

Equipment
Large pot

Serving Suggestions
For a well-balanced and protein-packed meal, serve the beans with rice steamed in chicken broth, some fresh pineapple, and a green salad on the side.

Servings
4

Preparation Time
15 minutes

Total Time
45 minutes

Spicy Peanut Orzo

5	ounces orzo (rice-shaped pasta)
2	tablespoons peanut butter
3	tablespoons warm water
1	teaspoon sesame oil
2	teaspoons honey
2	teaspoons Sherry cooking wine
2	teaspoons white wine vinegar
2	teaspoons reduced-sodium soy sauce
1	teaspoon chopped peeled ginger root
½	teaspoon sesame seeds
1	jalapeño pepper, seeded (if desired) and minced
	Dash cayenne pepper (or to taste)
	Salt to taste

- In a large pot of boiling salted water cook the orzo until tender but still firm to bite. Orzo cooks fast so taste it every minute or so until it is done. Rinse under cold water and drain.

- Spoon the peanut butter into a medium bowl. Gradually whisk in the warm water, a little at a time, until it is all incorporated into a smooth sauce. Be sure to add the water gradually, or you will end up with a lumpy, watery mess.

- Add the sesame oil, honey, Sherry, vinegar, and soy sauce to the peanut sauce, and stir until blended. Add the chopped ginger, sesame seeds, and jalapeño peppers. If you want a spicier dish, leave some of the seeds in the jalapeños. Stir in the cayenne pepper and salt to taste.

- Add the orzo to the peanut sauce, and stir well. Chill for at least 2 hours.

- Before serving, stir in an additional tablespoon or two of warm water and more salt to taste. Serve at room temperature.

Soups

Creamy Tomato-Basil Soup

*This is reminiscent of the famous tomato-basil soup served at
La Madeleine French Bakery.*

2	cups canned diced tomatoes, drained (or fresh tomatoes, peeled, seeded, and chopped)
2	cups tomato juice
6	to 8 fresh basil leaves
½	cup whipping (heavy) cream
¼	cup butter
	Salt and pepper to taste

- In a large saucepan combine the chopped tomatoes and tomato juice over high heat. Bring to a boil, reduce the heat to medium, and simmer for 15 minutes.

- In a blender or food processor, purée the soup and basil leaves just until smooth, but not frothy. Be very careful when blending hot soup—use a low speed and put a kitchen towel or oven mitt on top of the blender lid because the hot liquid may splash up.

- Return the soup to the saucepan over low heat. Stir in the cream and butter. Season to taste with salt and pepper.

- Serve hot.

Equipment
Large saucepan
Blender or food processor

Servings
2

Preparation Time
10 minutes

Total Time
25 minutes

French Onion Soup

Equipment
Large saucepan
Baking sheet

Servings
2

Preparation Time
15 minutes

Total Time
30 minutes

2	tablespoons butter
2	small yellow onions, chopped
1	stalk green onion, chopped
1	clove garlic, minced
½	teaspoon sugar
2	tablespoons Sherry cooking wine
1½	cups chicken or beef broth
¼	cup white wine
	Salt and pepper to taste
2	small sourdough bread slices
½	cup Swiss or Gruyere cheese

- In a large saucepan melt the butter over medium-low heat. Add the yellow and green onions, garlic, and sugar. Sauté for about 6 minutes, until the onions are translucent and begin to turn golden brown.

- Add the Sherry and simmer until the liquid nearly evaporates, about 2 minutes. Add the chicken broth and wine, and simmer for another 15 minutes. Season to taste with salt and pepper.

- Preheat the broiler. Place the bread slices on a baking sheet and top with Swiss or Gruyere cheese. Broil, watching constantly, until the cheese melts and starts to bubble.

- Ladle the soup into serving bowls, and float a slice of cheese bread on top. Serve hot.

Light and Tangy Southwestern Soup

This soup is very fast and extremely healthy. You can add broken tortilla chips and shredded Jack cheese as toppings if you like.

2   cups chicken broth
1   cup canned diced tomatoes
½   cup fresh or frozen corn
½   teaspoon garlic salt
¼   teaspoon oregano
⅛   teaspoon chili powder
⅛   teaspoon pepper
     Lime slices
     Chopped cilantro (optional)

- In a medium saucepan combine the chicken broth with the tomatoes, corn, and garlic salt over high heat. Bring to a boil, reduce the heat to medium, and simmer for 5 minutes, stirring occasionally.

- Reduce the heat to medium-low. Add the oregano, chili powder, and pepper, and cook for an additional 5 minutes.

- Ladle the soup into serving bowls, and top with lime slices and chopped cilantro if desired.

Share a drink or eat salad out of the same bowl.

Equipment
Medium saucepan

Servings
2

Preparation Time
5 minutes

Total Time
15 minutes

Mushroom Bean Soup

Equipment	
Medium saucepan	
Small bowl	
Servings	
2	

Preparation Time
15 minutes

Total Time
35 minutes

1   tablespoon olive oil

1   cup chopped onion

2   cloves garlic, minced

8   ounces mushrooms, cleaned, trimmed, and sliced

½   teaspoon dried thyme

½   teaspoon dried basil

1   15-ounce can chicken broth

1   cup canned diced tomatoes, drained

¼   cup white or blush wine

1   15-ounce can white beans (Great Northern beans), drained

• In a medium saucepan heat the olive oil over medium-high heat. Add the onion and garlic and cook for about 3 minutes or until the onion starts to soften. Add the mushrooms and cook, stirring frequently, until the mushrooms start to turn golden-brown, about 5 minutes longer.

• Add the thyme, basil, chicken broth, tomatoes, and wine; bring to a boil. Turn the heat to medium-low, cover, and simmer for about 15 minutes.

• In a small bowl mash half of the beans with a fork until smooth. Add the mashed beans to the soup, and stir until blended. Stir in the remaining beans, and cook another 5 minutes or until the soup is heated through.

Classic Tomato Soup

This recipe is really easy to make and requires almost no attention. The soup is pretty healthy as is, but you can leave out the butter in the last step if you want a lower-fat version.

1	teaspoon olive oil
2	cloves garlic, minced
1	14-ounce can chicken broth
2	14-ounce can diced tomatoes, undrained
$\frac{1}{2}$	teaspoon salt
$\frac{1}{4}$	teaspoon pepper
1	teaspoon dried Italian seasoning (or use thyme, basil, or oregano)
2	teaspoons butter

- In a large saucepan heat the olive oil over medium-high heat. Add the minced garlic and cook, stirring constantly, for about 1 minute.

- Add the chicken broth, tomatoes and their juices, salt, and pepper. Bring to a boil. Reduce the heat to medium-low, cover, and let the soup simmer for about 20 minutes.

- Stir in the Italian seasoning. With a ladle or a measuring cup, scoop out about half of the soup into the blender. Purée for a few seconds, until the soup is blended but not frothy. Be very careful when blending hot soup—use a low speed and put a kitchen towel or oven mitt on top of the blender lid because the hot liquid may splash up. Pour the blended soup into a medium bowl.

- Repeat the blending with the other half of the soup. Pour both batches of blended soup back into the saucepan and return to medium-low heat.

- Stir the butter into the soup until melted. Let the soup simmer an additional 10 minutes.

- Serve hot.

Equipment
Large saucepan
Ladle
Blender
Medium bowl

Servings
2 to 3

Serving Suggestions
Serve with your favorite bread or dinner rolls and a block of your favorite cheese.

Preparation Time
10 minutes

Total Time
40 minutes

Joel's Zesty Zucchini Soup

Thanks to Joel Thomas for this delicious recipe. If the soup is too thick, add warm chicken broth to thin it out. You can also add chopped cooked chicken to the soup at the end of the recipe.

Equipment
Large pot
Blender or food processor
Large bowl

Servings
4

Preparation Time
15 minutes

Total Time
45 minutes

3	cups chicken broth
2	zucchini, sliced
2	small carrots, sliced
½	small yellow onion, sliced
½	potato, cubed
½	cup sliced broccoli stalk
1	celery stalk, sliced
6	ounces cream cheese, cubed
	Salt and pepper to taste
	Tabasco sauce to taste

- In a large pot bring the chicken broth to a boil over high heat. Add the zucchini, carrots, onion, potato, broccoli, and celery, and bring to a boil again.

- Reduce the heat to medium-low, and simmer until the vegetables are tender, about 30 minutes.

- In batches, transfer the mixture to a blender or food processor and purée. Be very careful when blending hot soup—use a low speed and put a kitchen towel or oven mitt on top of the blender lid because the hot liquid may splash up. Pour the hot soup into a large bowl.

- Blend in the cream cheese with a wire whisk until melted and completely blended. Season with salt, pepper, and Tabasco sauce to taste.

- Serve hot or cold.

Desserts

Cream Cheese Mints

Very creamy and rich—a holiday favorite! You could make these mints with any flavoring extract you like, such as orange, lemon, or cinnamon.

3	ounces cream cheese
½	teaspoon peppermint extract
	Food coloring (if desired)
2½	cups powdered sugar
⅓	cup sugar

- In a large bowl beat the cream cheese with a wooden spoon until softened. Add the peppermint extract and a few drops of coloring (if desired), and stir until thoroughly mixed.

- Add the powdered sugar in ½-cup increments to the cream cheese mixture, blending thoroughly after each addition. You may need to use a fork to finish mixing, because the mixture will begin to get stiff.

- Line a baking sheet with waxed paper. Roll the cream cheese mixture into ¾-inch balls. Place the sugar in a small bowl; roll the mints in the sugar to coat. Place the mints on the waxed paper and press with your thumb to flatten slightly.

- Alternatively, if you have candy molds, you can press the sugared mints into the molds, and unmold at once onto the waxed paper.

- Let stand at room temperature until firm and dry.

Equipment
Large bowl
Baking sheet
Waxed paper
Candy molds (optional)

Servings
50 mints

Preparation Time
25 minutes

Total Time
25 minutes

Equipment
Fondue pot or double
boiler

Serving Suggestions
Make it a delectable fon-
due evening by serving
Cheddar Fondue (p. 111)
as the main course and
chocolate fondue for
dessert!

Servings
2 to 3

Preparation Time
10 minutes

Total Time
10 minutes

Chocolate Fondue

You can use either chocolate chips or chocolate bars for this fondue.
Liqueurs we like to use include Grand Marnier (orange), Amaretto
(almond), or Kahlua (coffee).

1   tablespoon milk, brandy, or your favorite liqueur
3   ounces semisweet, milk, white, or dark chocolate
    Strawberries, chunks of green apple and banana, angel
    food cake chunks, marshmallows, and/or maraschino
    cherries with stems

- If you have a fondue pot, light its fuel canister (Sterno)
  on high. If you don't have a fondue pot, you can use a
  double boiler on the stove. Get some water boiling in
  the lower pot, and then set the upper pot in place.

- Pour the milk or liqueur into the pot and let it warm
  for about 5 minutes. It should be very warm, but not
  boiling. Add the chocolate and slowly stir until the
  chocolate has completely melted.

- Serve warm with fruit, cake, and marshmallows for
  dipping.

Exchange dinner gifts, like fancy chocolates
or pastries.

Grandma Ruby's Oatmeal Cookies

Grandma Ruby always had these oatmeal cookies waiting for us in the cookie jar when we visited each summer.

½	cup shortening
1	cup brown sugar
1	egg
1	teaspoon vanilla
2	cups oatmeal
1½	cups flour
½	teaspoon baking soda
1	teaspoon salt
1	teaspoon cinnamon
½	cup raisins
½	cup chopped nuts
¾	cup milk

- Preheat the oven to 375°F.

- In a large bowl combine the shortening and brown sugar, and beat with an electric mixer on medium speed until thoroughly creamed together. Add the egg and vanilla, and beat until light and fluffy.

- In another large bowl mix the oatmeal, flour, baking soda, salt, cinnamon, raisins, and nuts until combined.

- Gradually add the dry ingredients to the creamed mixture, alternating with the milk. You may need to mix by hand instead of with the electric mixer if the dough gets too thick.

- With a spoon scoop out balls of dough about the size of small walnuts (about 1 inch in diameter), and drop onto an ungreased baking sheet.

- Bake for 15 minutes. Remove from the oven, let cool on the baking sheet for about 3 minutes, and then remove to a wire rack to finish cooling.

Equipment
Two large bowls
Electric mixer
Baking sheets
Wire cooling racks

Servings
36 cookies

Serving Suggestions
Serve with a tall glass of cold milk.

Preparation Time
15 minutes

Total Time
30 minutes

Dad's Lemon Meringue Pie

The peaks of the meringue turn a tantalizing golden brown in the oven—perfect for plucking off the pie by sneaky fingers. Beware of peak thieves!

Equipment
Rolling pin
Pie plate
Large bowl
Electric mixer

Servings
8

Preparation Time
20 minutes

Total Time
35 minutes

2	cups graham cracker crumbs
⅓	cup butter, melted
½	cup lemon juice
1	teaspoon grated lemon rind
15	ounces sweetened condensed milk (lowfat or nonfat is fine)
2	eggs, yolks separated from whites
¼	teaspoon cream of tartar
4	tablespoons sugar

- Preheat the oven to 325°F.

- In a plastic zipper bag finely crush the graham crackers with your hands or with a rolling pin. Pour the crumbs into a medium bowl and add the melted butter. Stir with a fork until evenly mixed.

- Press the crumbs into the bottom and up the sides of a 9-inch pie pan to form the crust. Alternately you can use four 4-inch tart pans. Chill the crust in the freezer while you make the filling.

- In a medium bowl combine the lemon juice and rind; gradually stir in the sweetened condensed milk. Add the egg yolks and stir well. Pour into the chilled crust.

- In a large bowl add the cream of tartar to the egg whites and beat with an electric mixer until stiff peaks form. Add the sugar gradually, and beat until the meringue is stiff and glossy.

- Pile the meringue onto the center of the pie. With a table knife carefully spread the meringue to the edges of the crust, using outward strokes. Make sure the

Attempt to speak with a French or Italian accent all night.

whole pie is covered. Ideally, it should form a "seal" with the edge of the pie plate.

- With the knife pull up little peaks in the meringue. Bake for 15 minutes, until the peaks are light golden-brown.

Make any meal special with a glass of sparking water and juice, mixed in equal parts: non-alcoholic bubbly!

Perfect Chocolate Chip Cookies

Doc, who is not that into sweets, devoured these cookies, declaring them "practically perfect." Our secret is melting part of the butter.

1	cup (2 sticks) butter, room temperature
¾	cup brown sugar, packed
¾	cup white sugar
2	eggs
2	teaspoons vanilla
2¼	cups white flour
1	teaspoon baking soda
1	teaspoon salt
1	12-ounce package good-quality semisweet chocolate chips (such as Ghirardelli or Guittard)

- Preheat the oven to 375°F.

- In a small saucepan set on low heat, slowly and carefully melt ½ cup (1 stick) of the butter. Don't let it burn!

- In a large bowl combine the melted butter, room temperature butter, brown sugar, and white sugar. Beat with an electric mixer at medium speed for 3 to 4 minutes, until the mixture is creamy and turns a little lighter in color.

- Add the eggs one at a time to the mixture, and mix until completely incorporated. Stir in the vanilla.

- In a separate large bowl stir together the flour, baking soda, and salt until combined. Gradually add the dry ingredients to the butter/sugar mixture, beating until completely combined and smooth.

- Add the chocolate chips. Stir gently until the chips are distributed evenly throughout the cookie dough.

- With a spoon, scoop out balls of dough about the size of a small walnut (about 1 inch in diameter), and drop onto an ungreased baking sheet.

*Have a picnic on a blanket in
the grass in your backyard.*

• Bake for about 10 minutes, until the cookies are beginning to turn golden brown (bake about 2 minutes
  longer if you prefer crisp cookies). Remove from the
  oven, let cool on the baking sheet for about 3 minutes,
  and then remove to a wire rack to finish cooling.

*Open the curtains when a storm is blow-
ing in and watch the lightning while you
eat by candlelight.*

Apple Cheesecake Torte

A springform pan is a baking pan with a removable bottom and a clasp that lets you loosen or tighten the sides. It can be found at any kitchen supply store or department store. This recipe recommends overnight chilling of the torte, so plan ahead.

Topping:

4   large Granny Smith apples
$\frac{1}{3}$ cup sugar
$\frac{1}{2}$ teaspoon cinnamon
$\frac{1}{4}$ teaspoon nutmeg

Crust:

$1\frac{1}{2}$ cups flour
$\frac{1}{2}$ cup chilled unsalted butter, cut into small pieces
$\frac{1}{3}$ cup sugar
$\frac{1}{2}$ teaspoon cinnamon
1   teaspoon vanilla
Dash of salt

Filling:

8   ounces cream cheese, room temperature
$\frac{1}{4}$ cup sugar
$\frac{1}{2}$ teaspoon cinnamon
1   large egg
1   teaspoon vanilla

- Preheat the oven to 400°F. Wrap the outside of a 9-inch springform pan with aluminum foil.

- Rinse the apples and remove the peels with a vegetable peeler or sharp paring knife. Cut the apples into quarters, remove the cores, then cut into slices. In a medium bowl toss the apples with the sugar, cinnamon, and nutmeg. Set aside.

- In a large bowl combine the ingredients for the crust. Using your fingertips, mix thoroughly (pinching the butter into smaller and smaller bits) until moist dough clumps form. Gather the dough into a ball. Press onto

Equipment
9-inch springform pan
Vegetable peeler or sharp paring knife
Three large bowls
Electric mixer

Servings
8

Serving Suggestions
This really doesn't need any embellishment, but if you like you can serve it with a dollop of unsweetened whipped cream.

Preparation Time
30 minutes

Total Time
2 hours (plus overnight chilling time)

the bottom and 1 inch up the sides of the prepared pan.

- Bake the crust until it is light golden, about 10 minutes. Remove from the oven. Reduce the oven temperature to 350°F.

- Meanwhile, in a large bowl combine the ingredients for the filling and beat with an electric mixer until smooth. Pour the filling into the crust and smooth it flat with a knife. Arrange the apple slices on top of the filling in a neat pattern.

- Bake the torte until the crust is golden brown, about 1 hour and 20 minutes. Remove from the oven and let cool at room temperature for 1 hour. Cover with aluminum foil and refrigerate overnight.

- When ready to serve, run a table knife around the pan sides to loosen the torte. Remove the pan sides. Serve the torte chilled.

You have overeaten when you are too full to have sex.

Autumn-Spice Apple Pie

This pie uses packaged puff pastry dough as a crust—almost as good as a homemade crust, and it's a real time saver. Puff pastry dough is available in the freezer section of most major supermarkets. Look for Pepperidge Farm brand.

$\frac{1}{2}$	cup raisins
$\frac{1}{4}$	cup dark rum
4	large Granny Smith apples
$\frac{1}{2}$	cup sugar
2	teaspoons cinnamon
$\frac{1}{2}$	teaspoon nutmeg
$\frac{1}{4}$	teaspoon allspice
$\frac{1}{4}$	teaspoon ginger
2	sheets (1 box) puff pastry dough
2	tablespoons cold butter
1	egg, beaten

- Preheat the oven to 400°F.

- In a small saucepan combine the raisins and rum over medium-low heat. Let simmer while you prepare the apples and pastry.

- Rinse the apples and remove the peels with a vegetable peeler or sharp paring knife. Cut the apples into quarters, remove the cores, then cut into slices. In a medium bowl toss the apples with the sugar, cinnamon, nutmeg, allspice, and ginger.

- With a rolling pin roll out one sheet of puff pastry to about 12 x 12 inches. Line the bottom and sides of a pie pan with the crust, with a little overhang all the way around. Once the crust is situated in the pan, fill it with the apple mixture, arranging the apple slices to lay flat in the pan.

- Drain the raisins and sprinkle them over the apples. Cut the butter into little bits and distribute it evenly

Equipment
Small saucepan
Vegetable peeler or sharp knife
Medium bowl
Rolling pin
Pie pan
Pastry brush

Servings
8

Serving Suggestions
Serve hot or cold with vanilla-bean ice cream and a sprinkle of cinnamon.

Preparation Time
30 minutes

Total Time
1 hour 15 minutes

Romance can never replace plain old-fashioned politeness. Saying "please," "thank you," and "I love you" are the most important parts of any relationship.

over the pie. With a pastry brush and water, wet the edges of the pastry.

- Roll out the other sheet of pastry to 12 x 12 inches, and lay it on top of the pie. Trim the excess from around the edges, and pinch the dough together to seal up the pie.

- With a sharp knife, poke a dozen or so holes in the top of the pie. Brush the beaten egg across the top of the pie with the pastry brush.

- Bake for about 45 minutes, or until the pastry is golden brown and slightly puffed. Remove from the oven and let cool slightly before slicing. Serve warm or cold.

Equipment
Vegetable peeler or small knife

Small bowl

Servings
2

Serving Suggestions
Spoon over ice cream or cake.

Preparation Time
10 minutes

Total Time
10 minutes

Drunken Strawberries

The strawberries can be eaten as is, or used as a topping on vanilla ice cream or on cake.

8	ounces fresh strawberries
1	tablespoon sugar
1	tablespoon brandy

- Rinse the strawberries under cool running water and gently drain. Remove the leaves and core from the strawberries with a small knife or the tip of a vegetable peeler. Cut the berries into slices.

- In a small bowl combine the berries, sugar, and brandy, and stir until the sugar dissolves. You can use the berries immediately, or chill for an hour in the refrigerator to let the flavors blend.

Make sure that your dining table is cleared of clutter, and you will be more likely to use it.

Gingerspice Caramel Ice Cream

This is our version of Ben and Jerry's "Festivus," a limited-batch flavor. We were very sad to see it go, and we knew we had to learn to make something similar to satisfy our inevitable future cravings! Plan ahead for this recipe, because you'll need to make a batch of cookie dough for it.

½	gallon premium vanilla ice cream (we like Blue Bell Homemade Vanilla)
2	teaspoons cinnamon
1	cup Crisp Gingersnap dough (p. 194)
1	small jar caramel sauce (about 8 ounces)

- Let the ice cream sit at room temperature for 10 to 15 minutes, until slightly softened. Scoop it out into a large bowl, add the cinnamon, and stir gently.

- Tear off teaspoon-size bits of the gingersnap dough with your fingers, and add them to the ice cream. Stir gently to blend.

- Spoon approximately one-third of the ice cream back into the tub or into a large plastic container. Drizzle one-third of the caramel sauce over the ice cream. Make two more layers of ice cream and caramel. Cover the container tightly with the lid or plastic wrap, and place in the freezer for at least two hours to harden.

Note
Be sure to use pasteurized eggs to make the cookie dough for this ice cream since you will be eating it uncooked.

Equipment
Large bowl
Large plastic container or
    ice cream tub

Servings
8

Preparation Time
10 minutes

Total Time
2 hours 30 minutes
    (including freezing
    time)

Crisp Gingersnaps

The dough will need to be chilled for several hours prior to baking these cookies, so be sure to plan ahead. These cookies can also be cut into gingerbread men and decorated with icing and candies.

Equipment
2 large bowls
Electric mixer
Rolling pin
Cookie cutters, knife, or mouth of a glass
Pancake turner or other wide flat utensil
Baking sheets
Wire cooling racks

Servings
48 2-inch cookies

Preparation Time
30 minutes

Total Time
2 hours 40 minutes (including chilling time)

$\frac{1}{3}$	cup soft shortening
$\frac{1}{3}$	cup brown sugar
1	egg
$\frac{2}{3}$	cup molasses
$2\frac{3}{4}$	cups flour
1	teaspoon baking soda
1	teaspoon salt
2	teaspoons cinnamon
1	teaspoon ginger

- In a large bowl combine the shortening with the brown sugar, egg, and molasses and beat with an electric mixer until smooth.

- In a separate large bowl stir together the flour, baking soda, salt, cinnamon, and ginger.

- Gradually add the dry ingredients to the shortening mixture, stirring thoroughly, until a smooth dough forms. You may have to stop and beat in the dry ingredients by hand once the dough starts getting thick.

- Wrap the dough securely in plastic wrap, and chill in the refrigerator for at least two hours.

- Preheat the oven to 375°F. Lightly grease a baking sheet.

- On a floured cutting board or clean counter, roll out the dough to $\frac{1}{4}$-inch thickness with a rolling pin. Cut into shapes with a knife or cookie cutters, or for round cookies you can use the mouth of a glass. (For crisper cookies, roll the dough to $\frac{1}{8}$-inch thickness.)

- Carefully lift the cookies from the counter with a pancake turner or other wide flat utensil, and place 1 inch apart on the prepared baking sheet.

Talk about what you'd like to do on your next vacation.

- Bake for 9 to 10 minutes (7 to 8 minutes for $\frac{1}{8}$-inch thick cookies), or until no imprint remains when lightly touched. Remove from the oven, let cool on the baking sheet for about 3 minutes, and then remove to a wire rack to finish cooling.

Use candles at the table whenever possible.

Mom's Cinnamon Rolls

We eat these for breakfast even more often than we eat them for dessert.

Equipment
2 large bowls
Electric mixer
2 8-inch cake pans
Rolling pin
Wire cooling racks
Medium bowl

Servings
10

Preparation Time
50 minutes

Total Time
4 hours 15 minutes

2	cups lukewarm milk
$\frac{1}{2}$	cup sugar
2	teaspoons salt
2	packages dry yeast
2	eggs, beaten
$\frac{1}{2}$	cup shortening, softened
7	to $7\frac{1}{2}$ cups white flour
$\frac{1}{2}$	cup melted butter
1	cup brown sugar
1	tablespoon cinnamon
$\frac{1}{2}$	cup pecans or walnuts, finely chopped (optional)
$\frac{1}{2}$	cup raisins (optional)

Icing:

$\frac{1}{4}$	cup butter or 2 ounces cream cheese
1	teaspoon vanilla extract
	Powdered sugar
	Milk

- In a large bowl combine the milk, sugar, and salt. Add the dry yeast; stir until dissolved. Let sit for 5 minutes, until the yeast bubbles to the surface.

- In another large bowl combine the eggs and shortening and beat with an electric mixer until smooth. Add the yeast mixture and mix well.

- Gradually add the flour in $\frac{1}{2}$ cup increments, mixing until a smooth dough forms. Knead until the dough is smooth and elastic. Place the dough in a bowl and let it rise, covered with a kitchen towel, in a warm place for approximately an hour, or until about doubled in size.

- Thoroughly grease two 8-inch round cake pans.

- On a clean surface roll the dough into a long rectangle with a rolling pin. Brush liberally with melted butter, and sprinkle with brown sugar, cinnamon, pecans or walnuts, and raisins.

- Roll the dough up, starting with a long side, so that a long narrow roll is formed. Slice the roll into 1-inch pieces and arrange in the prepared pans. It's OK if there is space between the pieces. Let rolls rise, covered with a kitchen towel, for about an hour, or until approximately doubled in size.

- Preheat the oven to 425°F.

- Bake the cinnamon rolls for 12 to 18 minutes, or until they just start to turn golden on top. Let the rolls cool in the pans for about an hour, then remove to wire cooling racks. When cool, frost with the powdered sugar icing.

- *To make the icing:* In a medium bowl beat the butter or cream cheese and the vanilla with an electric mixer. Add powdered sugar by the ½ cup and a few teaspoons milk, if necessary, to make a thick but spreadable icing.

Newfangled Seven-Layer Bars

Pepper gives this classic super-rich dessert bar a spicy kick. If cinnamon chips aren't available in your area, substitute more chocolate or butter-scotch chips.

Equipment
Small bowl
9 x 13-inch glass baking
   dish

Servings
24 bars

Preparation Time
10 minutes

Total Time
50 minutes

$1\frac{1}{3}$ cups sweetened flaked coconut

$\frac{1}{2}$ teaspoon pepper

$\frac{1}{2}$ cup butter, melted

$1\frac{1}{2}$ cups graham cracker crumbs

1   cup chocolate chips

1   cup butterscotch chips

$\frac{1}{2}$ cup cinnamon chips

1   cup pecan or walnut pieces

$1\frac{1}{3}$ cups sweetened condensed milk

• Preheat the oven to 350°F.

• In a small bowl combine the coconut flakes with the pepper.

• Pour the melted butter into a 9 x 13-inch glass baking dish. Sprinkle the graham cracker crumbs evenly in the pan, and layer the coconut mixture on top. In layers, add the chocolate chips, butterscotch chips, cinnamon chips, and nuts. Pour the sweetened condensed milk evenly over all.

• Bake for 25 minutes. Remove from the oven and let cool in the pan for 15 minutes. Cut into bars and serve.

Dim the lights during mealtime.

Mama Robin's Backstage Brownies

Robin Colleen Moore, a journalist/photographer, makes these brownies to bribe her way backstage after concerts so she can get interviews with the performers. They are actually THAT good!

1	cup sugar
¾	cup flour
⅓	cup cocoa
½	teaspoon salt
1	tablespoon instant coffee crystals
½	cup butter
2	large eggs
1	teaspoon vanilla
¼	cup water
6	to 12 ounces chocolate, butterscotch, and/or raspberry chips

- Preheat the oven to 350°F.

- In a large bowl combine the sugar, flour, cocoa, salt, and coffee crystals. Stir until well mixed. With a pastry blender or a fork, mix in the butter until the mixture forms small to medium-sized crumbs. It won't be entirely blended in—this is OK.

- Add the eggs, vanilla, and ¼ cup water, and stir until blended. The batter should be nice and thick, but still pourable. Add more water by the tablespoonful if necessary to get the right consistency.

- Stir the chocolate, butterscotch, and/or raspberry chips into the batter. Pour into an 8-inch or 9-inch square pan, and spread so it is even all the way to the sides.

- Bake for 30 minutes. Let the pan cool for at least 15 minutes before cutting and serving the brownies.

Equipment
Large bowl
Pastry blender (or fork)
8- or 9-inch square pan

Servings
16 brownies

Preparation Time
15 minutes

Total Time
1 hour

Pear and Yogurt Fruit Salad

This is an extremely fast and healthy breakfast or dessert, and one we eat quite often. It is high in fiber and low in calories. Add a little bit of sugar if you find the mixture too tart.

2	Bartlett or D'anjou pears
1	cup plain low-fat yogurt
2	teaspoons sugar (optional)

- Cut the pears into quarters, remove the cores, then cut into bite-sized pieces. Divide pears between two serving bowls.

- Add ½ cup yogurt and 1 teaspoon sugar (optional) to each bowl and mix well.

Equipment
Nothing special required.

Servings
2

Preparation Time
5 minutes

Total Time
5 minutes

☆Orange-Lemon Sorbet

Making homemade ice cream usually requires a lot of attention and special equipment, but not this sorbet. Simply mix, freeze, and blend until smooth!

1	medium orange
1	large lemon
2	cups orange juice (fresh-squeezed tastes best)
½	cup sugar

- With the fine holes of a cheese grater or with a citrus-zesting tool grate all of the peel from both the orange and the lemon, being careful not to grate any of the white pith.

- In a medium bowl mix the orange juice with the orange and lemon zest and sugar, stirring until the sugar is completely dissolved (this may take several minutes).

- Pour the mixture into an 8- or 9-inch round metal cake pan (or any other large metal pan). Freeze for six hours, or overnight.

- When ready to serve, crack the sorbet into pieces with a fork or kitchen knife. Put the chunks into a blender and blend, scraping down the sides if necessary, until smooth.

- Serve immediately.

Equipment
Cheese grater or citrus-zesting tool
Medium bowl
8- or 9-inch round metal cake pan (or any other large metal pan)
Blender

Servings
2

Serving Suggestions
Try the sorbet on top of slices of plain vanilla cake or angel food cake, and topped with some fresh berries.

Preparation Time
15 minutes

Total Time
6 hours 15 minutes (including freezing time)

Snickerdoodles

The dough will need to be chilled for several hours prior to baking these cookies, so be sure to plan ahead.

Equipment
Two large bowls
Electric mixer
Small bowl
Baking sheets
Wire cooling racks

Servings
5 dozen cookies

Preparation Time
20 minutes

Total Time
2 hours 30 minutes

1	cup shortening
2	cups sugar
2	eggs
2¾	cups flour
2	teaspoons cream of tartar
1	teaspoon baking soda
½	teaspoon salt
2	teaspoons cinnamon

• In a large bowl combine the shortening, 1½ cups sugar, and the eggs, and beat with an electric mixer until smooth.

• In another large bowl combine the flour with the cream of tartar, baking soda, and salt. Gradually mix the dry ingredients into the shortening mixture, combining thoroughly. Cover the dough and chill for at least two hours in the refrigerator.

• Preheat the oven to 400°F.

• In a small bowl mix together the remaining ½ cup sugar and the cinnamon.

• Using your clean hands, roll the chilled dough into balls the size of small walnuts (about 1 inch in diameter), and roll in the cinnamon-sugar to coat.

• Place the dough balls 2 inches apart on an ungreased baking sheet. Bake for 8 to 10 minutes, or until lightly browned. The cookies will still be quite soft, so let them sit on the baking sheet for several minutes after you take them out of the oven. Gently lift the cookies onto wire racks to finish cooling.

Menu Suggestions

One of the hardest things about cooking is trying to plan what to eat, especially if you are going for a meal complete with entrée, side dishes, and dessert. Here are some menu suggestions for full meals. As you become more familiar with the recipes, you can adapt these items to your own preferences.

Autumn Picnic in the Park

All these are foods that can be prepared ahead of time and kept cool or at room temperature, and eaten at the park without any silverware. Be sure to bring plenty of napkins or wet wipes, because the chicken can get a little messy.

- Debra's Simple Beer Bread (p. 66)
- Picnic Chicken with Sesame-Citrus Sauce (p. 96)
- Grilled Corn on the Cob (p. 167)
- fresh strawberries
- a chocolate bar to share
- your favorite wine or champagne

Spontaneous Picnic in the Park

What could be more romantic than to commemorate the anniversary of your first kiss with a moonlight picnic? This requires absolutely no cooking on your part. Just grab a tablecloth and some napkins, and stop by the supermarket or specialty grocery on your way out to the park.

- French baguettes
- an apple, a pear, some grapes
- three of your favorite specialty cheeses (try smoked Gouda, Welsh Harlech, Cotswold, Gruyere)
- fancy cookies or shortbread squares
- your favorite wine or champagne

Easy Sandwich Supper

You can make this tasty and filling meal in less than 30 minutes. It's great to eat in front of the TV while watching a rental movie.

- Quick Sliced Pork Sandwiches (p. 98)
- Baked French Fries (p. 159)
- Super-Fast Salad (p. 142) with Red French Dressing (p. 146)
- iced tea or soft drinks

Valentine's Day Dinner

This meal may look fancy, but it's really quite simple and quick to prepare. You will be sure to impress your partner with this array of delectable dishes, especially if you "fancy it up" by garnishing with parsley, snipped chives, or fresh flowers on the plate.

- Galveston Shrimp Cocktail (p. 50)
- Creamy Tomato-Basil Soup (p. 175)
- Lemon Herb Chicken (p. 99)
- Greek Rice Florentine (p. 165)
- Chardonnay wine

Light Summer Meal

This is a deliciously satisfying yet light meal, perfect for eating in the backyard on a nice summer evening. It's also a great meal for anyone who is watching their weight.

- Fresh Southwest Chicken Salad (p. 136) served on a bed of lettuce
- Light and Tangy Southwestern Soup (p. 177)
- Crisp Gingersnaps and vanilla frozen yogurt
- lemonade or hard cider

Fancy Italian Dinner by Candlelight

Sometimes you've just got to go all out for a fancy dinner. Maybe it's your anniversary or your partner's birthday, but whatever the occasion, dim the lights and break out the white tablecloth and real napkins, votive candles, and a CD of French or Italian bistro music. Serve wine both before and during dinner.

- Quick Bruschetta (p. 53)
- Super-Fast Salad (p. 142) with Lighter Lemon Vinaigrette (p. 149)
- Katy's Garlic Mushroom Red Sauce (p. 117) or Doc's Super-Secret Special Meat Sauce (p. 90) over angel hair pasta

- Sun-Dried Tomato Focaccia Bread with Olives (p. 67)
- Orange-Lemon Sorbet (p. 201)
- Chianti or Merlot wine

Bavarian Meal for Cold Nights

A hearty and filling meal, perfect for rainy winter nights by the fireplace.
- Speedy Sausage and Sauerkraut (p. 81)
- Spicy Potato Gratin (p. 169)
- Autumn-Spice Apple Pie (p. 190)
- sparkling apple juice

Southwestern Vegetarian Dinner

This menu can be adapted to suit the meat-lover's palate by adding chopped cooked chicken to the enchiladas. But we're willing to bet that carnivores won't even miss the meat in this tasty meal.
- Katy's Hot Salsa (p. 157) and tortilla chips
- Queso Fundido (p. 57)
- Light and Tangy Southwestern Soup (p. 177)
- Cheesy Onion and Mushroom Enchiladas (p. 130)
- your favorite south-of-the-border cerveza (beer)

Southwestern Vegetarian Dinner II

Though meatless, this dinner is hearty. Wear your sombrero and play Tejano or Mariachi music.
- Katy's Hot Salsa (p. 157) and tortilla chips
- Speedy Guacamole (p. 59)
- Magical Southwestern Black Beans (p. 118)
- Cilantro Rice (p. 162)
- Dad's Lemon Meringue Pie (p. 184)
- your favorite south-of-the-border cerveza (beer)

Easy Cleanup Fish Night

Sometimes the hardest thing about cooking fish is the smell. These recipes eliminate that problem and make clean-up easy, leaving you time for more important things.
- Super-Fast Salad (p. 142)
- Dad's No-Mess Salmon in a Packet (p. 73)
- Spicy Corn with Lime Cream Sauce (p. 172)
- Riesling or Pinot Grigio wine

Grilled Vegetarian Menu

Everything on this menu (except the ice cream) can be made outdoors on the grill. It's great for summer because it's not a heavy meal, and you don't need to turn on the oven or stove and heat up the kitchen.

- Hearty Grilled Tofu (p. 116)
- Grilled Vegetables (p. 170)
- Garlic Bread (p. 63)
- Gingerspice Caramel Ice Cream (p. 193)
- iced tea or soft drinks

East Asian Menu

If you don't already know how to use chopsticks, this would be a great opportunity to try them out! Sake is a Japanese rice wine, and it is best served hot.

- Teriyaki Scampi (p. 80)
- Grandma's Yaki Soba (p. 92)
- steamed rice
- fortune cookies
- jasmine or green tea or Sake

Homestyle Meal

Just like Mom used to make! Except that Mom probably didn't serve you beer with your meal, but we've added it for a grown-up twist.

- Flattened Oven-Fried Chicken (p. 91)
- Classic Potato Salad (p. 140)
- Mom's Baked Beans (p. 173)
- Perfect Chocolate Chip Cookies (p. 186)
- your favorite beer

Get-All-Dressed-Up-for-No-Reason Night

Get out of those sweatpants! Make a great meal memorable by celebrating in style.

- Crispy-Bottomed Salmon with Balsamic Sauce (p. 76)
- Doc's Sautéed Asparagus (p. 164)
- Lemon Olive Rice (p. 168)
- Drunken Strawberries (p. 192)
- sparkling water

Fondue Night

This is a meal to curl up with. Fondue cannot be rushed, so take your time and enjoy the meal. This meal should take you no less than two hours, perfect for a movie or for enjoying with friends.

- Cheddar Fondue (p. 111)
- Burgundy Mushrooms (p. 161)
- Chocolate Fondue (p. 182)
- your favorite beer or wine

Index

About Katy and Arushi

Katy Scott is a jack-of-all-trades creative type. She dabbles in the realms of writing, textile artistry, painting, sculpture, and digital design. She loves strange music, good food, and her beloved Macintosh computers. Katy lives in Dallas, Texas, with her husband, Murdock, a musician and graphic designer, and their two cats.

Fun fact: Katy is almost six feet tall, loves Doc Martens shoes, and has a uncanny ability to solve the most frustrating mind teasers.

Arushi Sinha has a degree in medical anthropology and works in the medical publishing industry. She loves to cook for her friends and family, make beautiful quilts, and travel to exotic places as often as possible. Arushi lives in Dallas, Texas, with her husband, Shyamal, a software engineer.

Katy and Arushi have been friends since they were ten years old.

Fun fact: Arushi has not owned a television set since 1994, by choice, and looks fabulous in fancy hats.

HILLSMAN STUART JACKSON

shopping lists   notes

_____   _____

_____   _____

_____   _____

_____   _____

_____   _____

_____   _____

_____   _____

_____   _____

_____   _____

_____   _____

_____   _____

_____   _____

_____   _____

_____   _____

_____   _____

_____   _____

shopping lists

notes

_____
_____
_____
_____
_____
_____
_____
_____
_____
_____
_____
_____
_____
_____
_____
_____

shopping lists

notes

shopping lists

notes

_____

_____

_____

_____

_____

_____

_____

_____

_____

_____

_____

_____

_____

_____

_____

shopping lists   notes

_____   _____
_____   _____
_____   _____
_____   _____
_____   _____
_____   _____
_____   _____
_____   _____
_____   _____
_____   _____
_____   _____
_____   _____
_____   _____
_____   _____
_____   _____

shopping lists   notes

Printed in the USA
CPSIA information can be obtained
at www.ICGtesting.com
JSHW052016140824
68134JS00027B/2502